THE ROCK ART OF
SOUTH AFRICA

THE ROCK ART OF SOUTH AFRICA

A. R. WILLCOX

with a foreword by
PROFESSOR J. DESMOND CLARK

NELSON

THOMAS NELSON AND SONS (AFRICA) (PTY) LTD
P.O. Box 9881
302-304 Barclays Bank Building
Commissioner and Kruis Streets
Johannesburg

THOMAS NELSON AND SONS LTD
Parkside Works Edinburgh 9
36 Park Street London W1
10 Warehouse Rd. Apapa Lagos
117 Latrobe Street Melbourne C1

THOMAS NELSON AND SONS (CANADA) LTD
91-93 Wellington Street West Toronto 1

THOMAS NELSON AND SONS
18 East 41st Street New York 17 N.Y.
SOCIÉTÉ FRANCAISE D'EDITIONS NELSON
97 rue Monge Paris 5e

Printed in the Netherlands in letterpress and photogravure by Vada, Wageningen.

Contents

Acknowledgements

Much of the extensive fieldwork necessary to the preparation of this book was made possible by grants for expenses from the South African Council for Scientific and Industrial Research to whom my thanks are gratefully given.

The work has been made pleasant by the kindness of the many friends my wife and I have made all over South Africa and the help and hospitality extended to us by farmers, game rangers, foresters and others, to many of whom we were strangers.

The staffs of the Africana Museum and Library of the Johannesburg Municipality and the Director of the Old Transvaal Museum, Pretoria have been helpful in every way possible to them. The aid of individual scientists of the C.S.I.R., of Dr H. B. S. Cooke and of the Diamond Research Laboratory of Johannesburg is gratefully acknowledged in the appropriate places in this book.

To Mr. Harald Pager I am indebted for bringing several new rock painting sites to my notice and for certain translations from the German made at my request which have aided my researches and to Mrs P. Carter (formerly Miss Pat Vinnicombe) for guidance to sites in the Underberg District.

To my fellow enthusiast, collaborator, assistant photographer, secretary and typist, i.e. my wife, I owe so much more than my thanks.

My debt to Mr A. A. Telford for his great care in making the maps and drawings will be apparent to the reader.

Acknowledgements and thanks are also due for permission to publish some of the illustrations and quotations, as follows:

Mr P. Anton Hendriks, Director of the Johannesburg Municipal Art Gallery, for his colour photograph of 'the White Lady' of the Brandberg, Plate 25. The Africana Museum, Johannesburg for Plates vi, vii and viii. The Rijks Museum, Amsterdam for Plate i. The British Museum for Plate xvi. The Librarian of the Library of Parliament of the Republic of South Africa for Figure 2. Professor Dr Reinhard Maack, Dr E. Scherz and the S. W. African Scientific Society for Plate xi. Mr Walter Battiss for the photograph from which Figure 38 was made. Dr. H. J. Heinz for Plate v. Methuen and Co. and Daniele Vare for the quotation at the head of Chapter 3. Mr. M. C. Burkitt for the quotation in Chapter 3. 'The Daily Sketch', London for Figure 42.

Except as otherwise acknowledged all photographs, colour and black-and-white, are my own.

Foreword

The prehistoric rock art of South Africa ranks with that of Western Europe and the Sahara among the richest and best preserved in the world.

Since the late twenties and early thirties of this century a number of beautifully illustrated volumes of reproductions of South African rock paintings and also of engravings has been published. These have served to show the vitality, beauty and wide variety of styles and techniques of this art, but they are all concerned with limited regions and, up to now, no comprehensive work on the art as a whole has appeared. This has rendered it difficult for all but the experts to gain a perspective view of the several great regional schools and their inter-relationships. Alex Willcox's present work is, therefore, all the more important in that it provides us with an excellently concise and extremely readable synthesis written by one of the leading authorities on the rock art of the Republic of South Africa and one who is a pioneer in the technique of reproducing the work of those amazing prehistoric hunting peoples - the Bushmen and their ancestors.

In his book *Rock Paintings of the Drakensberg* published in 1956 Alex Willcox showed how greatly superior is colour photography over tracing for reproducing the true nature of the art in relation to superposition, weathering and the rock wall. He has now extended his researches to include engravings also and, not being content with the flat, usually lifeless, results from a single tracing or rubbing, he has developed a new technique which has given a much more faithful reproduction than was previously possible. The result is a series of beautiful plates in colour and black and white that enable the reader to capture something of the associations of this art and the circumstances behind it, lying out as it does on a boulder-strewn dolerite kopje or hidden away in some cave or rock shelter opening on the hunting territory of the painter band.

This naturalistic art never ceases to astound one that it could have been produced by nomadic hunters little removed in their way of life from our Palaeolithic ancestors. The age of the art, however, has for long remained a matter of disagreement among prehistorians chiefly because of the absence of any *art mobilier* by which to connect the paintings or engravings on the rock with the cultural equipment of the artists preserved in the living places. In the critical hands of the author the dating evidence in favour of an age of not more than 1500 years for the surviving art is very convincing though it must be borne in mind always that the origins of the traditions from which these regional schools developed must of necessity extend back for several millennia earlier - probably to the beginning of the Later Stone Age in early post-Pleistocene times.

The author has as extensive a first-hand knowledge of South African rock art sites as any other single person and he and his wife have visited hundreds of these sites and discovered not a few new ones, besides rediscovering others that had been lost. To do so involved the Willcoxes in many miles of walking over the veld or climbing in the escarpments and kopjes of the central plateau. But the author has not been content merely to reproduce the art - he has done much more. Having analysed it from the point of view of the artist, prehistorian and ethnographer he gives an interpretation of its origins, history and associations which is the most complete and rational that has yet been attempted.

Always cautious and critical, Willcox has analysed in a masterly way the various regional schools and then gone on to demonstrate the associations of this art and to show us the artists themselves and the manner of their lives. To do this he has had to combine the functions of art critic, prehistorian and ethnographer, and his historical sketch of the latest Bushman artists and their way of life gives us a knowledge of the cultural relationships of the paintings and engravings that makes the art itself so infinitely more understandable and impressive.

This finely illustrated book shows the vital importance of the ethnographic approach to prehistoric studies in a continent where many of the social and economic practices depicted by the prehistoric artists are still to be found among the autochthonous hunting and gathering peoples of Africa who are their present day descendants.

J. DESMOND CLARK

KALAMBO FALLS
12th July 1963

Colour Plates

Black and White Plates

xii

Maps and Drawings

Introduction

'South Africa' in the title and text of this book means the Republic of South Africa, formerly the Union of South Africa, and its enclave the High Commission Territory of Basutoland. 'Southern Africa' includes also Northern and Southern Rhodesia, South West Africa, Swaziland and Bechuanaland.

As long ago as 1721 an ecclesiastic of the Portuguese Colony of Moçambique reported to the Royal Academy of History at Lisbon the existence in that colony of paintings of animals on rocks[1]. It was the first hint to the extra-African world of the prehistoric art, extraordinary both in quantity and quality, of central and southern Africa.

Not much later (1752) in South Africa the members of an exploratory expedition led by Ensign August Frederick Beutler found along the Fish River of the Eastern Cape many rock paintings which they recognised as the work of Bushmen though they called these people 'Little Chinese' because of their somewhat Mongoloid features[2]. Thus it was accepted in South Africa that people of Palaeolithic culture (as the Bushmen were, despite the date) could be accomplished artists, a century and a half before the savants of Europe finally accepted the validity of de Sautuola's discovery of the rock paintings of Altamira, after refusing for twenty years to believe in their true antiquity on the grounds that such art could not be the work of Stone Age savages.

The first known copies of rock paintings of South Africa were made by Johannes Schumacher, in 1776 or 1777 somewhere in the south or west of the Cape[3]. The next known copies were made in the Sneeuwbergen of the Eastern Cape North of Graaf Reinet by a member of Governor Joachim van Plettenberg's expedition of 1778. Accompanying the expedition was Captain Robert Jacob Gordon, later Colonel and Commandant at the Cape. He was a competent artist, so it was either he or some unknown artist also present who made the copies. They were not published and the original watercolours are in the Rijks Museum, Amsterdam. By kind permission of the Museum one of the copies is reproduced in Plate i. Apart from a single drawing of the head of a beast (thought to be a unicorn) in John Barrow's *Travels in the Interior of Southern Africa in the Years 1797 and 1798*, it was not until 1837 that the first copies of rock paintings were published. These were from sites near Oudtshoorn (see Plate 13) and were reproduced in colour in Sir James Alexander's book *A Narrative of Exploration among the Colonies of Western Africa*.

Works by E. Holub[4], L. Peringuey[5], M. Helen Tongue[6], O. Moszeik[7], J. P. Johnson[8], F. Christol[9], J. V. Zelizko[10] and M. C. Burkitt[11] followed; but it was only with the publication in 1930 of George William Stow's copies (made 1867–1878)[12] that any widespread interest was aroused outside Africa. Since then many books and papers have appeared notably by Dorothea Bleek[13], Maria Wilman[14], C. van Riet Lowe[15, 16], E. Goodall[17, 18], L. Frobenius[19, 20], W. Battiss[21] and others, to add to the now extensive literature, although no work has yet attempted to cover the whole field of prehistoric art in South Africa. It is important that this be done, as

1

many of the problems concerning the art can be fairly judged only with regard to the whole of the evidence. Hence this book.

G. W. Stow deserves to be better known and more honoured especially in his own country, South Africa, for he was not only the first to study the rock art seriously and make a large collection of copies, but also a great pioneer in many other ways. As ethnographer, palaeontologist and explorer he made notable additions to knowledge, as geologist his discoveries included the Vereeniging coal fields upon which great steel and chemical industries are now based. While he was making copies west of the Drakensberg, and beginning only five years later, another explorer-artist, Mark Hutchinson with his son Graham was seeking out and copying rock paintings on the Natal side of the Berg. Their copies are mostly in the Natal Museum, Pietermaritzburg, and the Library of Parliament, Cape Town. Among the latter is the pen and ink drawing reproduced by kind permission of the Parliamentary Librarian as Plate ii. It is dated 1876 and is of great interest as there were still Bushmen in the Drakensberg at that time and the drawing may have been made from life. At least the Hutchinsons must have found many rock shelters just as the Bushmen left them.

Thanks mainly to the above mentioned works most educated people the world over now know of the existence, at least, of 'Bushman paintings' but few know anything of the other prehistoric art of South Africa, the pictures cut into the koppie rocks. Partly no doubt because of the difficulty of satisfactory reproduction, this other art has, in comparison with the paintings, been sadly neglected and for this reason will be given full consideration here. Although it is a more variable art, including much that is crude and clumsy, the best of the petroglyphs equal any examples of the painters' art, ranking indeed as masterpieces by any standards.

In recording and reproducing rock art for publication the most important thing, in the present writer's view, is that the reader should get a true impression of how the work looks on the rock. This is why photography, especially in colour, is preferable to tracing or artist's copies where it is practicable. If complemented by careful tracing so much the better.

Photography however is seldom applicable to the rock engravings. The cut and uncut surfaces at best differ only slightly in tone and often the engraving is barely visible. Except in a few cases colour photography therefore has little advantage, if any, over black and white and the latter often does not yield a photograph clear enough for satisfactory reproduction. It is easy to take a latex mould of the work and from it make a plaster cast but this is no more photogenic than the original, (in fact rather less so) unless the lines or the whole area within the outline are then artificially darkened or coloured in. It then looks quite unlike the petroglyph as it is now and – unless there has been much good guessing – unlike the work as it originally was when the artist stepped back to admire his completed handiwork. Usually a good rubbing can be made, often revealing lines not visible on the rock and this can be reproduced but it will also show many natural markings on the rock to detract from the artist's conception. The method finally adopted when direct photography was impracticable has been to take a rubbing, then to photograph it and make a print of the desired size thus retaining the correct proportions. This the illustrator Mr. Allen Telford transferred by tracing to drawing paper, and with the rubbing and where possible, also a photograph direct from the rock before him, filled in the rock background by stippling. This method it is thought gives as true an impression of the engraving *as it originally was*, as is possible without full colour reproduction which, as remarked above, would involve some guessing as to what the colours were. But photographs have also been included (some in colour) to give the reader an impression of the engravings as they look now. We have gone further and, obtaining the cooperation of sculptor Zoltan Borbereki, have recreated a line engraving on a rock taken from a Maanhaarrand site. In this case the colours must be right as the cortex is only about two millimetres thick and the original artist, like the modern one, must have cut through it to expose the blue rock (see Plate 27).

The student of the petroglyphs (as of the paintings) finds great divergence of expert opinion regarding the age and authorship of these works of art. There is no doubt that it was Stone Age art, executed (except perhaps for a few of the latest works) by people in the hunting and foodgathering stage of culture. There is no doubt either that the latest were done within the last couple of centuries or that the earliest were executed centuries earlier. But how much earlier? The late Professors C. van Riet Lowe and A. J. H. Goodwin were both inclined to believe – neither considered it more than a fair probability – that the earliest engravings were the work of men of the Middle Stone Age (see chapter 1) which would give them an age of several thousands of years. Miss Maria Wilman, who studied the engravings more thoroughly than anyone else has yet done, and who wrote the only major work on the subject[14], believed on the other hand that six hundred years was the outside limit. This figure was suggested also by Dr. Emil Holub[4]. As to the artists, some believe them to have been Bushmen, some do not, and those who do differ as to whether the painters and the carvers were of different branches or tribes or the same people adapting their art to the circumstances of different terrain. Some also wish to attribute the paintings or some of them to peoples other than the Bushmen – to Hottentots, Bantu or others.

The difficulty is that the evidence at present available is mostly indirect and its appraisal requires the most delicate weighing of the probabilities by unbiased minds.

In this book the evidence will be reviewed and a new approach attempted: that is to look at the whole picture of the distribution of the prehistoric arts and stone industries of Southern Africa, to put forward evidence and expert opinion on the rate of weathering of the stone, to compare the two arts of painting and engraving and to suggest some inferences.

The writing of this book was completed when the news reached us of the death of the Abbé Henri Breuil, doyen of prehistorians and virtual founder of the comparative study of prehistoric art. My disagreement with him on a number of points expressed in this book and already made known in my other writings in no way lessens my admiration for his achievements and my file of amicable correspondence with him will always remain one of my most valued possessions.

I

Some Background Facts

The rationale of the distribution of the rock art becomes clear only if considered in relation to the geomorphology of the country. Other problems involve considerations of climate, petrology and general archaeology. This chapter aims to review the elementary facts of the subjects – as far as relevant to South Africa and to our theme – for the benefit of the new-comer to such studies. The informed may safely skip it.

A glance at a physical map of Southern Africa reveals a fairly simple configuration. A continuous escarpment roughly parallel to the coastline, highest in the East and gradually decreasing in height as it turns westward and northward, defines the plateau which forms the interior of the subcontinent. Between this scarp and the south coast, fold ranges delimit the great karoo, little karoo and coastal plain. Backing the great escarpment in the east (there called the Drakensberg) at its highest part lies the mountain massif of Basutoland. The table-land thus formed declines gradually from east to west and as the rain-bearing winds of this summer rainfall area come from the north-east the country grows progressively drier towards the west until it becomes semi-desert (the Kalahari). The nature of the climate of the plateau has an important bearing on the problem of the age of the petroglyphs and must be considered in more detail later.

Underlying the basalt which forms the tops of the escarpment of the Drakensberg and the Maluti Mountains of Basutoland, is a deep bed of sandstone. Wherever this bed is exposed it weathers in a peculiar way to form overhangs or rock shelters and has therefore been given the name Cave Sandstone, though few of the rock shelters are deep enough to deserve the name of caves. Other sandstones and mudstones of the Stormberg and Beaufort Series to the south of the Cave Sandstone weather similarly.

The Table Mountain sandstone of the mountains of Southern and South-Western Cape Province and the Waterberg sandstone and granite of the Northern Transvaal also form rock shelters. Limestone in a few places forms true caves, such as the famous Cango Caves near Oudtshoorn and the dolomite Wonderwerk Cave near Kuruman. In the rock shelters of all those regions and at the mouths of the caves mentioned paintings are to be found. Indeed with little qualification it is true to say that they are found in rock shelters wherever these occur in Southern Africa outside heavily forested areas and with rock not impossibly rough.

The map (Fig. 1) summarises diagrammatically the physical features above described and shows also the limits of the Cave Sandstone except for isolated exposures in the extreme north of the Transvaal. Fig. 2 shows the areas in which most of the rock art is found, something like 95 per cent of it falling within the hatched areas. Except for a very few engravings (perhaps half a dozen sites) zones 1, 2, and 3 contain paintings only and zone 4, with equally few excep-tions, contains only petroglyphs. However, where zones 2 and 4 overlap, naturally both

4

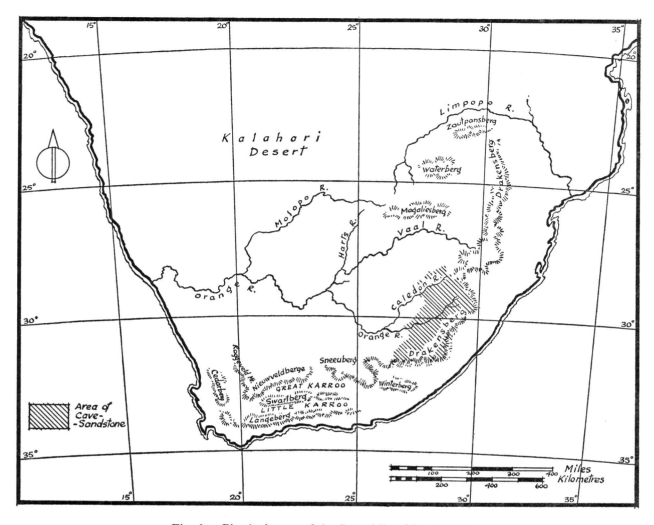

Fig. 1. Physical map of the Republic of South Africa

paintings and petroglyphs occur. It will at once be seen how closely the painting zones correspond to the mountain (rock shelter) areas and how the petroglyphs are restricted to the 'high-veld' and 'middle-veld' plateau.

The publication *The Distribution of Prehistoric Rock Engravings and Paintings in South Africa*[16] compiled by the Archaeological Survey of the Union (now Republic) of South Africa lists 1,592 'localities' having rock paintings, 340 having rock engravings and 6 with painted engravings. 'Locality' means a farm, Nature Reserve, Forest Reserve, or similar area, and as these are often large the number of *sites* is certainly greater. The remarkable segregation of paintings and petroglyphs will be appreciated from the fact that zone 4 as marked on the map (Fig. 2) contains well over 300 engraving sites and except for the overlapping area zone 2 has only two or three painting sites. In contrast, about 75 per cent of the painting sites of the Republic (therefore about 1,200) occur in zone 2 but the same zone, excluding the overlap has only *two* engraving sites. This does not take into account the painted engravings, all of which are doubtful.

5

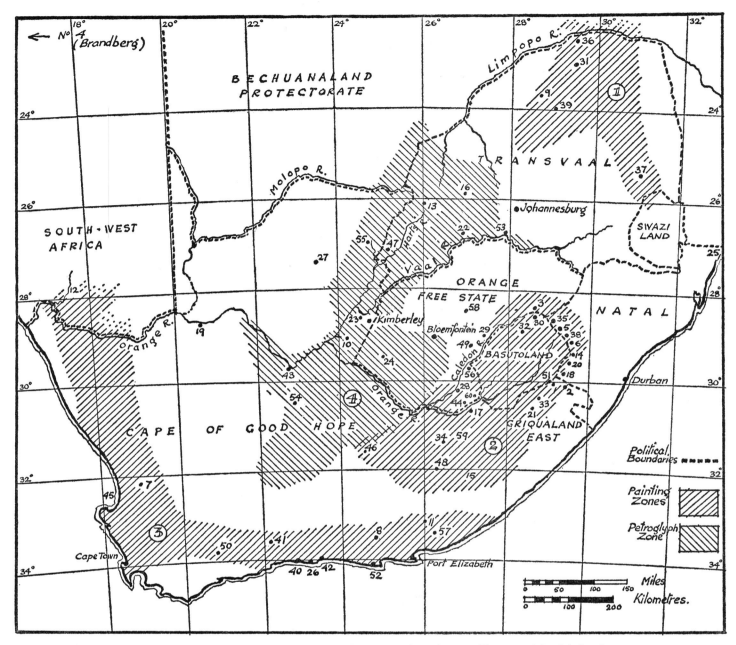

Fig. 2. Map to show the art zones of South Africa and the sites referred to or illustrated in this book.

As already noted the paintings in zones 1, 2, and 3 occur in rock shelters and in the very few cases where paintings occur on engraving sites – as at Vosburg, Cape Province – they also are in rock shelters of a kind, very small ones formed by the overhangs of boulders. Apart from these shelters, if such they can be called, I know of no rock shelters in zone 4. If there are any they must be very few. The petroglyphs on the other hand are found on the surfaces of rocks on open sites usually on or near the tops of low hills * (Plate iv).

The difference of siting between the paintings and engravings must be considered in more detail in a later chapter. So also must the differences in style between the paintings of the three zones in which they occur, for the local variations are considerable and it is relevant to this study to enquire which bears the closest resemblance to the petroglyphs.

* For notes on recently discovered petroglyphs in a rock shelter in zone 1, see Chapters 6 and 11.

KEY TO MAP OF ART ZONES

SITE	NO. ON MAP	SITE	NO. ON MAP	SITE	NO. ON MAP
Bambandyanalo	36	Kamberg	20	Prieska	43
Bamboo Mountain	18	Kenegha Poort	21	Redan	53
Bellevue	1	Kinderdan	55	Rockydrift	37
Beersheba	2	Klein Aasvogel Kop	44	Rose Cottage	29
Bethlehem	3	Klerksdorp	22	Rouxville	44
Bosworth	22	Klipfontein	23	Royal Natal National Park	35
Brandberg	4	Koffiefontein	24	St. Helena Bay	45
Caledon Poort	3	Kosi Bay	25	St. Theresa Mission	32
Cathedral Peak	5	Knysna	26	Sneeubergen	46
Cathkin Peak	6	Kuruman	27	Snow Hill	18
Clanwilliam	7	Kwartelfontein	28	Sweitzer Reneke	47
Clarens	3	Ladybrand	29	Tabamyama	14
Cockscomb Mountain	8	La Rochelle	30	Tarkestad	48
Cradock (farm)	9	Leeuwfontein	59	Thaba Phatshwa	49
Doornhoek	16	Lorraine	7	Tradouw Pass	51
Doornkloof	16	Maanhaarrand	16	Tsoelike River	50
Driekopseiland	10	Makabene Mountains	31	Tynindini	17
Ebusingata	35	Makhetas	32	Underberg	18
Eland Cave	6	Matatiele	33	Uysberg	29
Ezelzacht	41	Matjes River	42	Vaalbank Spruit	58
Fish River (Eastern Cape)	11	Meads	33	Vereeniging	53
Fish River (South-West Africa)	12	Molteno	34	Vosberg	54
Game Pass Valley	20	Mont-aux-Sources	35	Vryburg	55
Genaadeberg	60	Mpongweni	18	Warrenton (see Kimberley)	
Gestoptefontein	13	Mpungubwe	36	Wepener	56
Giant's Castle	14	Nelspruit	37	Willow Grove	59
Great Kei River	15	Ndedema Gorge	38	Wilton	57
Groot Moot	16	N'Kosisana Stream	6	Winburg	58
Halfway House (see Kimberley)		North Brabant	39	Wodehouse	59
Harmony	33	Oakhurst	40	Zastron	60
Herschell	17	Orange Springs	29	Zitzikama	52
Himeville	18	Oudtshoorn	41	Zuurfontein	34
Ikanti Mountain	18	Plettenberg Bay	42		
Kakamas	19	Pniel (see Kimberley)			

The rock art of South-West Africa is beyond the scope of this book but it should be mentioned that petroglyphs occur there also as well as paintings. The two arts are not there geographically separate as in South Africa but the same rule – paintings in rock shelters, petroglyphs on exposed rocks – is found to apply. The petroglyphs are extremely crude, badly drawn and coarsely cut, and there is no reason to believe that there is any direct cultural connection between them and the fine art of the Republic.

It will be necessary also to refer to the divisions of the Stone Age in South Africa. By general consent the prehistoric period in Southern Africa before the introduction of metals is divided into an Earlier Stone Age, Middle Stone Age and Later Stone Age[22]. These are based upon typological differences with ample confirmation from stratigraphy. Transitional periods are now also recognised, the first between the Earlier Stone Age and the Middle, the second between the Middle and the Later Stone Age. The duration of the three main periods is much less certain; reasonable estimates are 8,000 years for the Later, 40,000 years for the Middle and 400,000–500,000 for the Earlier.

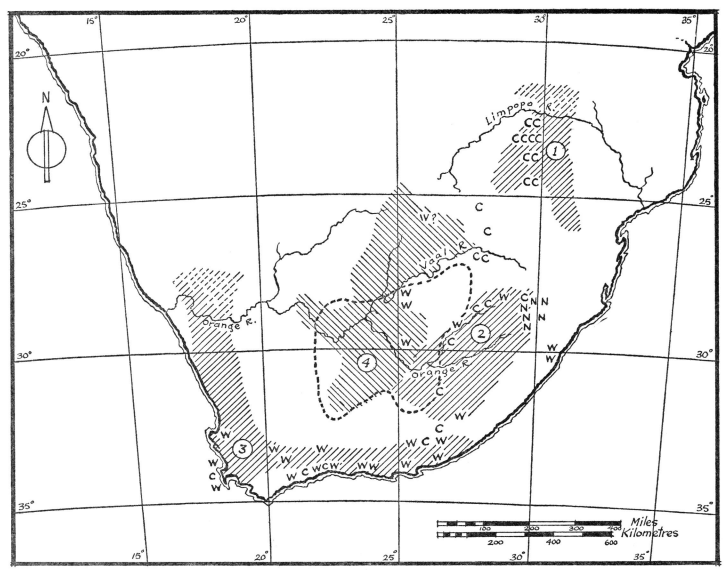

Fig. 3. Map to show the distribution of Later Stone Age industries in South Africa. The broken line on the map surrounding a large part of zone 4 includes all the Smithfield B sites (about 100) except a few outliers and a few Smithfield A sites. W. means Wilton, C means Smithfield C, N means Smithfield N (see pages 9 and 60).

The typology of the Earlier Stone Age need not concern us in this book, nor need that of the Middle Stone Age except to say that the material is easily recognisable by an expert and readily distinguishable from Later Stone Age artefacts. It is necessary however to say more about the industries of the Later Stone Age. These have been divided by the pioneer work of the late Professors A. J. H. Goodwin and C. van Riet Lowe into two *Cultures*, the Smithfield and the Wilton, which were, at least in their last phases, contemporaneous. The Smithfield Culture has been subdivided into 'A', 'B' and 'C' phases, an 'N' variation and other local variations. Artefacts of the B, C, and N industries were being made until the introduction of metals into the areas in which they are found or the extinction of Stone Age Man in those regions. The C phase of the Smithfield resembles the Wilton so closely that it is distinguishable only by the presence of microlithic *crescents* (tiny artefacts shaped like a segment of an orange) in the Wilton and the present writer would prefer to classify the Smithfield C as *Crescentless Wilton*. Also it

8

seems to him that it would be more realistic to postulate one *culture* to which all the paintings, probably all the petroglyphs, and of course all the stone implement industries associated with them, could be assigned. For the purposes of this book, however, the traditional terminology has been used.

Figure 3 shows the distribution of the Later Stone Age industries in relation to the pre-historic art. No complete distribution map exists and new sites are constantly being found but the general pattern of distribution as shown here is unlikely to require much revision.

2

The Bushmen – Their Origin and Culture

As it is certain, for reasons which will later appear, that the Bushmen were the authors of most of the prehistoric art of South Africa – if not indeed of all of it except some easily recognisable crude Bantu work – it is necessary to outline briefly in this and the next chapter the facts as far as known of their origin and rise, their culture before it was modified by contact with alien newcomers, their struggle for survival, their defeat, decline and fall.

'Bushman' is a word to use with care for it connotes a physical type, a way of living, and a language. The people to whom it was originally applied (and whose descendants linger in the Kalahari still) were described by the early colonists as 'little people', 'of small stature' and as living by hunting and gathering wild foods, and keeping no domestic animals[24], this, in clear distinction both physical and cultural to the Hottentots who were described as of medium or good stature and as keeping cattle and sheep[25, 26]. Scientific studies later revealed other physical differences (e.g. of skull form) and marked differences of language. The culture known to have been practised by the historic Bushmen may for all we know have been shared by people very different physically.

'Bushman' as a noun therefore should be used only in reference to the short-statured hunter people historically known and still in sadly reduced numbers surviving, whereas 'Bushman' as an adjective may describe the culture and language of quite other people who lived as the Bushmen did. If this is born in mind the meaning of 'Bushman painting' for example will be clear.

The other Bushman racial characteristics are well known. Delicately built with tiny hands and feet, but wiry and deep chested, they are capable of astonishing feats of speed and endurance. The skin colour is yellowish, the hair sparse and in tightly spiralled tufts ('peppercorns'), the eyes slanting and with an additional eyelid fold (the epicanthic fold) which gives them an oriental look, the ears almost lobeless, the face orthognathous or only slightly prognathous, with low forehead bulging rather than receding and fairly prominent cheekbones. The spine, curved inward near the base (lumbar lordosis), increases the often great prominence of the buttocks caused by deposits of fat (steatopygia) which also occur on the thighs (steatomeria). In the women there is gross elongation of the labia minora. Shared only by their racial kin the Hottentots, and among them much less common, is the position of the penis, which stands out almost at right angles to the vertical. Several other of these peculiarities, e.g. steatopygia and lordosis, were shared by the Hottentots in varying degrees. The word 'race' has so many meanings that it may be thought to mean nothing but if used in reference to the Bushmen it should, because of these similarities, include also the Hottentots as the Bush-Hottentot or Khoisan race. The Bushman is better considered a sub-race.

The origin of the Bushmen as above defined is a matter still debated by the physical

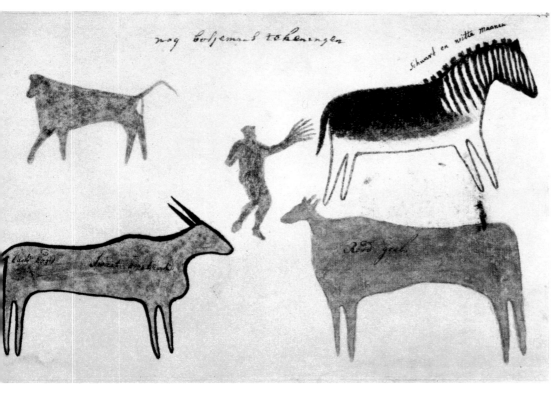

nog bossemans tekeningen

schwart en witte maanen

Red goed

i. One of the earliest copies of rock paintings in South Africa, made in the Sneeubergen by a member of Governor Joachim van Plettenberg's expedition of 1778, probably Robert Jacob Gordon, later himself Commandant at the Cape.

ii. A Bushman shelter in the Drakensberg, from a pen and ink drawing by Mark Hutchinson, 1876. Probably a reconstruction, but possibly from life.

iii. A small rock shelter at the Meads near Matatiele, Griqualand East. It has fine paintings on its ceiling.

iv. Typical petroglyph sites. One in the immediate foreground and another (Bosworth Farm) at the top of the hill.

v. A Bushman and his young wife in the Kalahari. She exhibits lumbar lordosis and steatopygia.

vi. This picture well illustrates the different ways of life of Hottentots and Bushmen. The former are on trek with their possessions loaded on their cattle and the Bushmen hunters are hiding from them. In the distance a Bushman disguised as an ostrich is stalking a flock of the birds. An advance party of Hottentots is erecting their portable huts. From the Sloman Collection in the Africana Museum, Johannesberg.

vii. This picture, also from the Sloman Collection, shows a scene enacted repeatedly during the long conflict between Bushman and frontier farmer. The Bushmen have captured some cattle and are driving them back to their mountain fastness. Some of their number ambush the pursuing farmers and are ready to let loose stones and arrows. One beast failing to make the climb is being killed to discourage the pursuers. Note the arrows worn in a band around the Bushmen's heads so that they can be quickly snatched and shot.

anthropologists. In these complex matters the non-specialist would prefer to accept authority but finding that the principal experts differ he can only acquaint himself with their conflicting views and, however ill qualified to judge, form his own tentative opinions.

The basic questions of physical anthropology relevant to the problems of the prehistoric art are: 1. how long has the Bushman physical type existed? 2. did that type evolve in Southern Africa or migrate here from North Africa or further afield? – and 3. what are the reasons for the physical peculiarities of the Bushmen? The questions are obviously interrelated and the conflicting theories are by no means mutually exclusive.

Recent research has added little that helps to determine the time of the first appearance of the Bushmen in South Africa. Indeed we 'know' a great deal less than we did ten years ago, for Bushman or 'Bushmanoid' skulls from Zitzikama and Matjes River in the Cape, and others from elsewhere, formerly believed to date from the Middle Stone Age are now considered, from a more critical study of their provenance to be of the Later Stone Age[27]. Even the presumed ancestor of the Bushman, Boskop Man, is under attack, for his skull was unearthed by labourers in 1913 before the days of controlled archaeological digging and although apparently the remains were found about four feet below the surface they might well have been interred from a higher level, as Dr. Singer has pointed out[28]. A single stone implement assigned by Professor C. van Riet Lowe to the Middle Stone Age, was found in circumstances not precisely known somewhere near the calveria. It may have nothing to do with it as there are large areas in the Boskop vicinity and elsewhere in South Africa where, if you dig a hole at random you are quite likely to find a Middle Stone Age implement.

It seems that at present there are no known Bushman or even Proto-Bushman skeletal remains that can be certainly assigned to the Middle Stone Age. Remains which do appear to be of that age or earlier are much larger than, and in other ways not much resembling, the Bushmen. Sometime in the Later Stone Age therefore the Bushmen appeared in South Africa: which brings us to the second question.

In spite of the doubtful presence of putative Middle Stone Age ancestors in Southern Africa, Professor L. H. Wells and Professor P. V. Tobias, leading authorities on this question both argue for the local evolution of the Bush type, the former from 'the basic African Homo Sapiens' and the latter from 'the Rhodesioids' akin to Rhodesian or Broken Hill Man, a Neanderthaloid type probably dating from about the beginning of the Middle Stone Age, i.e. about 50,000 years ago[29].

Professor Tobias's theory has raised the objection that the evolution of the Bushman from such a radically different type of man could not happen in a time so short when measured by the evolutionary time scale. Professor Wells's derivation of the Bush type from a much older stock allowed on the other hand plenty of time for the change. Professor Tobias, however, pointing to the immense diversification of dogs in a mere 10,000 years, ranging in size from the Great Dane to the Chihuahua, claims that evolution can be very fast when Natural Selection is reinforced by Cultural or Sexual Selection and that in this combination of evolutionary pressures lies the reason for the Bushman's rapid emergence *and the reasons for his physical peculiarities*.

This brings us to the third question but before passing on to that it should be mentioned that not all South African anthropologists have accepted the theory of a local evolution of the

Bushman. The late Dr. Robert Broom held the belief that the Bushman arrived, more or less fully evolved, from the far north of Africa or the Near East. Professor Dart's views will be summarised later in this chapter.

As for the racial traits of the Bushman, here again we feel less certain than we did a few years ago when they were confidently believed to be adaptations to the desert conditions in which the Bushmen now live. The steatopygia for example was, like the camel's hump, a reserve of fat on which the body could draw in times of starvation, conveniently located where it would not interfere with rapid movement; the small stature resulted in a lesser need for water, and so on. To aquire such adaptations would certainly require thousands of years of desert living and Tobias points out (quite correctly) that the Bushmen are known, on unassailable grounds, to have inhabited medium and high rainfall areas as well as the semi-desert. It is indeed somewhat doubtful whether they lived in the Kalahari at all, except perhaps seasonally after rains, before they were driven into it in the last few centuries by hostile newcomers, Hottentot, Bantu and European. Who would? To this the far north school of thought could rejoin that the Bushmen might have acquired these adaptations in another desert – the Sahara – before migrating southwards, and that the Kalahari was once vastly larger than it is today. Professor Tobias, however, denies that they are adaptations specifically to desert conditions, admitting them only to be advantageous in any hunter people in any African habitat. Small size, he says, seems to be an advantage in Bushmen today, the taller men being comparatively clumsy hunters, consequently less respected and, it is implied, less sought after as sexual mates. Big buttocks in the female he accepts as serving the practical purpose of food storage against times when children must be born and suckled in spite of the occasional food shortages inevitable in the hunter's life; but besides this, Tobias argues, they conferred greater sexual attractiveness on their possessor and hence tended to be perpetuated in a larger number of children. This is the normal process of sexual selection. (One could perhaps find a parallel in the Hollywood cult of quite other female protuberences.) There is one objection to Professor Tobias's attractive theory. Do any Bush women, however ill-endowed posteriorly, remain unmated, more particularly do they bear fewer children than their more glamorous sisters? If so this would clinch the argument, if not it would destroy it.

If I may venture to make an original suggestion by way of further complicating the question it seems to me not impossible that high female fertility and a tendency to accumulate fat on the body may well have gone together as the result of the same glandular activity.

Selection, natural or sexual, can of course act only on the material subjected to it. It is a sieve which passes or rejects but cannot originate changes. These arise spontaneously in the germ plasm as 'mutations' to be selected for perpetuation or discarded. The small stature of the Bushman could have arisen from the occasional occurrence of such dwarfing mutations selected as explained above, but a mechanism less direct seems much more likely. This is the emergence of an hereditary tendency (also by mutation and selection) for certain juvenile characteristics, including shortness, to be retained after puberty. This theory explains also the beardlessness of the adult Bushmen, their large-headedness in proportion to body size, and many other skeletal features considered juvenile. It may also explain their imagination, artistic gifts and zest for living and it implies no adverse criticism of their intelligence, for this faculty – in contrast to knowledge, skill, and experience – does not increase after about the

12

age of fourteen. We are justified therefore in thinking of the Bushmen as a race of Peter Pans – the race that never grows up.

Many people, indulging in biological snobbery, consider the Bushmen to be 'degenerate'. There is no foundation for this view. They are on the contrary highly evolved, perhaps the most highly evolved people on earth, and the retention of juvenile traits in adulthood, found in differing degree in all human races when compared to other species, is carried a stage further in the Bushmen. If therefore in this respect the European is highly evolved, the Bushman is more so.

Professor M. R. Drennan has argued this point in a fascinating paper in which he also points out that many of the juvenile traits e.g. beardlessness and more delicate skeletal structure, may equally be considered feminine characteristics transferred to the adult male[30].

Having written the above I showed it to Professor Raymond Dart who was kind enough to give me his views. While not wishing to engage in controversy over the origins of the Bushman type he thought there was a larger measure of agreement among the physical anthropologists than I had indicated, and that some of the apparent divergences of opinion would disappear if the scientists concerned would first agree on the definition of their terms. He adheres to the 'Boskop Man' concept.

> 'The nearest living relations of the Bush type', said Professor Dart,' are the Pygmies of Central Africa, and these people were well known to the Egyptians who found them as far North as the Southern Sudan. Amongst the Bushmen are Boskop types of people. The Sandawe and Hadzapi peoples of Tanganyika have Bush-Hottentot characteristics and still speak click languages. Skulls of Bush (or Pygmy type) are known from Egypt, Kenya, Tanganyika, and from both Northern and Southern Rhodesia. So there is little doubt that 2,000 years ago a distribution map of the African races would have shown the Bush (or Pygmy) race in direct contact with the Brown Race in eastern Africa and few if any Negroes among them but many Boskop people'.

Although Professor Dart considers the big-headed people from the caves of Zitzikama, Matjes River, and elsewhere in South Africa to be variants of the Boskop type, he holds them to be forerunners rather than ancestors of the Bush type.

> 'This Boskop type', he added, 'has persisted and formed the essential population at Mapungubwe in the Northern Transvaal and the major element in the Hottentot population along the Orange River and the Strandloper around the southern coast; it is also prevalent among the Southern Kalahari Bushmen.
> 'It was representatives of the Brown Race of Egypt and Mesopotamia who brought to the Bush-Boskop peoples first the Later Stone Age and later the Neolithic cultural elements',

concluded the Professor. I am glad to record his views although I find them largely unacceptable especially his equating of the 'Bush' and 'Pygmy' types and his allegiance to the 'Boskop' concept which now seems to me about as real as the still lingering smile of the departed Cheshire Cat.

As regards the northern or southern origin of the Bushmen the truth may lie somewhere between the extreme views. Early waves of movement perhaps pre-Bushman *culturally* may have taken place in either direction so that the race may for a long time have occupied both ends of the continent. A much later movement perhaps of a small group may have brought

13

such cultural elements as the bored stone, the bow, and graphic art, even the technique of making microlithic implements. Since the use of the bow and the first appearance of micro-lithic implements appear to have been earlier in the north, and the appearance of rock art certainly was so, there can be no doubt that the movement was from north to south. The view held by some that these cultural elements could all have been independently invented at both ends of Africa I find quite unacceptable especially in respect of the bow and arrow, a far more ingenious device than is generally realised. The movement could have taken place by cultural diffusion only, the ideas being gradually passed on from tribe to neighbouring tribe of hunters, or by the slow random movements of one people, and in either case may well have taken thousands of years to reach South Africa. For myself, in the present state of science, I find it easier to believe that the culture was brought by the people found in possesion of it or their immediate predecessors the so-called proto-Bushmen; but having arrived it could have been passed on to other peoples through hybridization or culture contact. Similarly, the peculiar elements of the historical Hottentot culture e.g. the keeping of cattle and sheep may (much later) have been brought – in this case unquestionably from the north – by a group of people who then mingled with differing physical types already here to produce the heterogeneous people found sharing the Hottentot culture when Europeans first colonised the Cape.

Fortunately – for the present bemused writer – the origins of the Bushmen do not vitally concern the study of South African prehistoric art for it is common ground that whether they evolved in the north or south of the continent they or closely related 'Bushmanoid' peoples occupied most of Southern Africa, except the heavily forested areas, for many centuries before the pastoral Hottentots and the Bantu arrived.

Their culture, it has already been said, was non-pastoral and non-agricultural, the natural resources of the veld alone providing their food and their whole equipment. Hunting and fishing secured their protein requirements, but their very varied diet included innumerable varieties of berries and other fruits, bulbs, roots and nuts, seeds, insects, ant and termite eggs, birds' eggs, shell-fish, honey, etc. Some of these were sources of liquid also (or at least they are now), e.g. the body fluids and stomach contents of animals and the juices of fruits such as the tsamma melon. Although a hard struggle in their latter days and now, their life must have been easy enough before being disrupted by newcomers, for the earliest travellers found immense herds of game roaming the still unravished veld in the Bushmen territories.

Their habitations were natural rock shelters where these were found and small crude shelters of branches elsewhere; their clothing, loin cloths, aprons and cloaks (karosses) of animal skins, their ornaments, beads made from ostrich eggshell, bands of leather or rings of ivory about their limbs, or simply body paint. Having to trek whenever, because of local drought or over-hunting, the game became scarce, the Bushmen kept their equipment to a minimum in quantity and weight. A typical camp would have, in addition to clothes and ornaments, only the womens' digging sticks and the spheroidal bored stones which weighted them, leather bags to contain the collected food, calabashes, ostrich eggshells or the sewn-up skins of small animals as water containers, probably an upper and nether grindstone for crushing seeds, melon pips, etc. and perhaps a crude pot or two. There would also be the men's bows and arrows, quivers, knob-kerries, fire-sticks and painting equipment. Stone implements for cutting up and skinning their kills, for scraping the skins and for wood working (e.g. making bows and arrows and knob-kerries) would lie about but would not be transported when trekking, others being made in a few seconds when required.

The short weak Bushman bow with its bow-string of twisted sinew, the quiver made of leather or by hollowing out a section of a branch of Aloe Dichotoma, and the reed arrows, are too well known to need further description here. The arrow heads were most commonly of bone and latterly formed by a small triangle of iron beaten flat, but a few perfect tanged and barbed stone points have been found and there is good historical evidence that arrow heads were also made of laurel-leaf shaped points and by a pair of *crescents* placed together and cemented to the foreshaft with vegetable mastic. These were barbed with quills, thorns or small splinters of stone. The minutest crescents might have been used thus. It is difficult to see any other use for them. The poison spread behind the point was from many sources including snake venom, spiders, grubs of a certain insect and the juices of various plants.

The curious implement often seen in the rock paintings made by fixing a jackal's tail to the end of a short stick, which served various purposes from wiping perspiration from the brow, to swatting flies and signalling, was commonly used also by Hottentots and Bantu.

Naturalists to a man the Bushmen had names for the flora and fauna of their environment and knew well the habits of the animals, birds, and insects, and the properties as food, medicine, poison and perhaps as paint media, of the plants. They had even discovered a plant which by its smell would keep lions away[31, 32]. They were geologists enough to know where to find the minerals from which they made pigments and the best stones for making implements; and they were astronomers enough to name the principal stars and planets and know their peculiarities. As meteorologists they became renowned rain-doctors. In short they had an impressive body of practical knowledge and knew their environment better than most civilised men know theirs.

Their amusements were dancing, mime, music, storytelling and the graphic arts. Rhythmic clapping accompanied the dances which often took the form of one or a few dancers dressed in the skins of animals miming their actions, sometimes solely for entertainment, but sometimes no doubt, also for ritual and magical purposes, as in the case of the eland bull dance of the Naron (Fig. 4).

Bushman hunting and fishing methods will be described in a later chapter as will also be their mythology.

Contrary to common belief the Bushmen's lives, like those of all 'savages', were as circumscribed and regulated by as many rules and tabus even as ours are. Etiquette rigidly controlled the behaviour of each member of the group in relation to the other members and was especially strict between married people and their spouse's parents. Elaborate rules also governed the cutting up and distribution of the killed animals. In the Cape Bushmen studied by Dr. Bleek and Miss Lloyd children could not eat the jackal's heart, or the tip of the springbok's tail or some parts of the ostrich; unmarried men and women must not eat a certain kind of tortoise, no women must eat the flesh of the lynx, and so on.

Puberty ceremonies differed widely among the tribes. All tribes had such rites for girls but only the northern tribes for boys. The ceremonies involved segregation, hardship, usually some minor physical mutilation such as scarification and finally a rite of acceptance as adult members of the group.

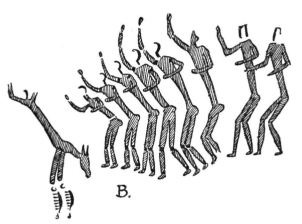

Fig. 4. Bushman Dances
A Orange Springs O.F.S. Men perform the Mantis dance while women clap the rhythm.
B N'Kosisana Stream, Drakensberg, Natal. Dancer wears an antelope's skin and spectators gesticulate.
C Abel's Cave, Drakensberg. Performer wearing animal's skin mimes while seated figures look on, some clapping.

Social grouping was elastic, each group consisting normally of a few families but in times of plenty such as the tsamma melon season much larger groups would form, indulge in feasting, dancing, and general merry-making, and eventually split up again.

Marriage ceremonial was simple but the process of courtship could be long, with much bringing of gifts to the girl's family. These had usually to include the best parts of animals hunted and killed by the suitor alone, to prove his competence to support a family. On his acceptance by the girl and her family the man took the bride to his hut, gave a feast for both families and the couple's friends, and the matter was settled.

But the temptation must be resisted to go into the details of Bushman culture further than is relevant to the interpretation of the rock art and beyond what is necessary to indicate the character of these people. The reader is referred to the Bibliography (page 000) for further reading and especially to Schapera's *The Khoisan Peoples of South Africa*[33].

Two examples of these people's ingenuity taken from more recherché sources deserve to be better known. These are their methods of signalling and food preservation. Their remarkable discovery of inoculation against snake bite was described in my *Rock Paintings of the Drakensberg*[34].

They could convey definite messages by three systems – by waving their karosses in prescribed ways[32, 34] by smoke signals[31], and at night by the use of fires[35]. Their way of preserving animals' flesh (at least in Basutoland) was to separate the fat from the lean, boil the former, and dry the latter very thoroughly, pound to a powder and keep fat and lean in separate containers. Mixing them together and boiling when required made a quick and nutritious meal[36].

One other feature of their culture must be restated for it was the chief cause of their conflict with the white man. Ownership of land was an idea foreign to their minds, but hunting rights and water rights were quite another matter. For one Bushman group to hunt in another's territory, use their waterhole, or even to collect eggs or vegetable food there, was tantamount to a declaration of war and was expected to be taken as such. Considering this the Bushman was on the whole forebearing when the European blundered through slaughtering the game often far in excess of his food requirements for 'sport' – a reason for killing also foreign to the Bushman mind.

Their character is best summed up in the words of the late Dorothea Bleek, daughter of Dr. Bleek and honorary reader in Bushman languages at the University of Cape Town, for probably no European has known them better than she: 'the Bushman is a good lover and a good hater, very loyal and very revengeful. He remains all his life a child, averse to work, fond of play, of painting, singing, dancing, dressing up and acting, above all things of hearing and telling stories'.

3

The Bushmen – Their History in South Africa

'The Master taught us that it is best to take our troubles as they come and where
they come. And this is how he Himself learnt that lesson. He was travelling with His
disciples, when He came upon a woman weeping beside a newly made tomb. He
asked her:
"For whom do you mourn?"
And she answered: "for my son!"
The Master looked round and beheld other tombs. And he asked who was buried
there. The woman answered.
"My husband and daughter."
"And how did they die?"
"They were also killed by a tiger."
"If the tigers are so dangerous in these parts,
Why don't you go away and live elsewhere?"
And the woman answered:
"The Government does not trouble us much here." '

A traditional story of Confucius, retold by Daniele Vare in '*The Gate of Happy Sparrows*'

As the sad history of the Bushmen – that is their story in the written record – has been often
told, it will not be recounted in much detail here, but it is often relevant to the dating and
interpretation of a work of rock art to know approximately when the first Bantu or European
entered the area in which it is found, and when the Bushmen were exterminated or driven out.

The ethnic picture when van Riebeeck's three ships sailed into Table Bay in 1652 to found
the first European settlement at the Cape is in many respects obscure. In their slow drift
southward the Bantu had on the east coast a century before reached the southern end of what
is now Natal[37]; by 1600 they had reached the Great Fish River but went no further, no doubt
because they found the Hottentots in occupation of the lands to the west.

Hottentots, at least seasonally, occupied the Western as well as the Southern Cape, sharing
their territory with Bushmen. The latter were in the hills, while the Hottentots with their
cattle and sheep kept to the plains. The Namaqua Hottentots, whose territory ranged from
about 200 miles north of the Cape to north of the Orange River, were in contact with a Bantu-
speaking people to the north-west, and in 1661 were at war with them. These people, the
Briqua, the late Professor A. J. H. Goodwin identified with the BaThlaping[38]. Theal called
them Bechuana. Their frontier with the Namaqua lay somewhere between the Kalahari desert
and the Orange River: it is not possible to be more definite.

The situation further north is also far from clear. We know by carbon dating that at
Bambandyanalo adjoining Mpungubwe just south of the Limpopo a non-negroid 'Bush-
Boskop' cattle-owning people were living at least as late as c. 1400 A.D.[39]. It is debatable
whether their culture more resembled that of the Hottentots or that of the Bantu-speaking

18

1. Alex and Nancy Willcox painting hunting in the Drakensberg. Baby daughter Sandra is being carried by our Hlubi maid. This excursion was successful, some fine and previously unknown paintings being found in the rock shelter seen in the photograph. (See Plates 23 and 24).

2. A painted shelter at Snow Hill, Underberg, Natal. The waterfall and weaver birds' nests help to make this a delightful living place.

3. Beersheba Farm, Griqualand East. Fight between farmers and Bushmen cattle thieves. For description see Page 23. The scene is 3 feet from top to bottom.

4. Kwartelfontein, near Smithfield, Orange Free State. One of the few paintings showing Europeans. They wear late 18th century or early 19th century dress and carry muskets with powder horns at their belts. To the left a bad painting of a horse and below, some lions. The human figures are about 10 inches high. (See page 25.)

5. Kwartelfontein. Cattle and a fat-tailed sheep show that these paintings must be contemporaneous with or later than the Europeans in Plate 4. The sheep are about 4 inches long.

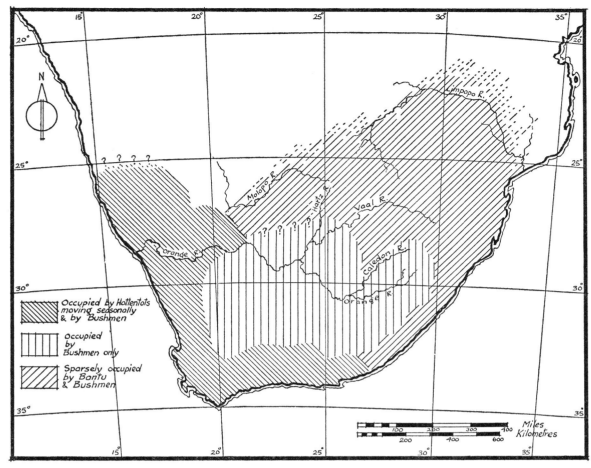

Fig. 5. Map to show the ethnography of South Africa, circa 1652.

people as historically known, and what language they spoke is of course beyond knowing. They may have been overwhelmed or simply by-passed by the Negroid Bantu on their way south. For the time of the Bantu crossing of the Limpopo we are dependent on tribal genealogies passed on orally from generation to generation, and guesses as to the average 'reign' of the chiefs. Ellenberger, using this method, places the date between 1400 and 1500 A.D.[40], Bryant makes it about 1300 A.D.[41]. The obvious weakness of the method, apart from its general vagueness, is that you never know whether you have reached the earliest time of occupation of a particular region; the tribe whose oral tradition takes you furthest back may have displaced an earlier tribe whose traditions are for ever lost. Even 1300 A.D. is more likely therefore to be too late an estimate rather than too early.

By our reference date of 1652 some Bantu, the Le Ghoya and BaFoking, were living in what are now the northern and eastern parts of the Orange Free State and about this time the first Bantu tribe to live in Basutoland moved into the Caledon River valley and the region immediately to the east. This was the Amazizi, a N'guni tribe who came from the foothills of the Drakensberg in Natal. The whole of Natal, Griqualand East, Pondoland and the Transkei between the sea and the Drakensberg foothills was Bantu territory. The rest of South Africa was the hunting ground of the Bushmen, surely a fine estate for a people never very numerous (see map, Fig. 5).

The subsequent history of the Bushmen is a story of retreat, with fierce resistance at every

19

step, as the hostile aliens closed in on all sides. Relations with the Bantu, however, were at first amicable. The people initially were few, the country vast. Their way of life did not unduly disturb the Bushmen who liked the hills where the rock shelters are, while the Bantu with their animals preferred the plains. The newcomers were glad to learn from the resident sages the properties of the local plants, the ways of the animals, the weather signs. 'The Bushman' runs the Basuto proverb 'is the teacher'. Often the Bushman in his cave in the hills became the rain-doctor for the neighbouring Bantu. This seems to have happened in Rhodesia at the painted cave of Domboshawa as Mr. M. C. Burkitt recorded:[11]

> 'A tradition exists among the local Bantu natives to-day which connects this cave with the production of rain. In fact the place is really a sacred spot and, until recently, in times of drought pilgrimage was made there to obtain rain. The method of procedure was to bring offerings to the cave and wait there for some time until the sign that the offerings had been accepted and therefore that rain would come appeared. The sign took the form of smoke issuing from the top of the great round granite dome of the hill itself, in the side of which the rock-shelter opens. The mechanics of the phenomenon would seem to have been due to the following circumstances. At the back of the rock-shelter are the beginnings of a huge fissure which apparently continues through the rock right away to the top of the hill, forming, as it were, a sort of chimney. Under certain conditions the smoke from a fire lit in the cave would be drawn up this fissure or chimney and would issue out at the top of the mountain. This would only take place when the wind was blowing from a particular direction, i.e. from the east, whence rain normally came. This explains why the suppliants often had to wait a considerable time before their requests were granted, even when all the necessary ritual performances had duly taken place. They had to wait, indeed, till the wind went round to draw the smoke up to the top of the mountain, and, incidentally, to bring up the clouds.'

A similar belief attaches to another painted cave in the north-west Transvaal where until very recently (possibly even now) Bantu sent up offerings of food to the cave when rain was needed, although the Bushmen have been ousted from the neighbourhood for nearly a century[114]. The same thing happened in the Transkei[32, 121] and Pondoland.

In the latter territory indeed the Bushmen achieved a very satisfactory arrangement with the Bantu Pondomise tribe which persisted late into the nineteenth[114] century. Elders of the tribe in 1883 deposed to a Government Commission the following:

> 'Bushmen are believed to have the power of bringing rain from the heavens and cattle are often sent to them as an application for rain. They also have the right of collecting a small share of the crops after harvest is over, which is a thanksgiving for the rain they bring from the heavens, which enables the people to reap plenty of grain.'

Heads the Bushmen won, tails the Bantu lost!

The most famous South African rain-maker of all, Majaji, chieftainess of the BaLovedu and origin of Rider Haggard's *She*, was fair-skinned and may have got her colour and her weather lore from a Bushman parent.

In the Soutpansberg of the Northern Transvaal a custom still lingers from the days when Bushman magicians had to be propitiated or bribed. The Bantu there, mostly BaVenda, when they go to a place where there are rock paintings must leave some offering, usually now a bangle or piece of cloth. The old MuVenda who guided me to one site dared not himself disregard the custom and somewhat sheepishly left a fragment of cloth. Asked why, he could not or would not, say. It was just the thing to do. Scores of bangles and oddments already placed there immediately under the paintings showed that Bantu not infrequently visited the spot, perhaps still to ask for rain, perhaps, since the bangles indicated more women visitors than men, to pray for babies.

Only when the Bantu and their domestic animals became too numerous, and the game as a consequence too scarce, did the two ways of life become incompatible and conflict inevitably break out. By this time much intermarriage had usually taken place. In some places e.g. Bechuanaland and the Lake Chrissie region of the eastern Transvaal, Bantu-Bush relations have remained amicable to this day. In the latter place even European-Bush relations have remained friendly.

The first encounter of Europeans with Bushmen took place in 1655 some 50 *mijlen* (nominally 230 miles but probably much less) north of Cape Town[24], and they were often met with subsequently by exploring parties in all parts of the Southern and Western Cape. With the white men it was war almost from the first. Their way of life and the Bushman way were hopelessly incompatible. The Europeans as they spread inland, and especially in the dry karoo, sought out the springs and waterholes on which they and their livestock must depend. But these were equally necessary to the game upon which the Bushmen preyed, which shy animals, or at least those not slaughtered by the newcomers, then moved away. The Bushman must follow in perpetual retreat or must instead shoot the new strange animals he found grazing in his hunting grounds and watering at his spring. He chose the latter course, considering this his immemorial right, thereby evoking bitter reprisals from the settlers. The ensuing war lasted some 170 years and was fought with increasing savagery on both sides. It was frontier war, parallelled in many parts of the world, in which both sides were as usual convinced of the rightness of their cause and in which neither side could give way without abandoning its basic livelihood. One incident from Stow which took place in the Sneeuwberg Mountains north of Graaf Reinet sufficiently illustrates the spirit of the conflict[31].

'After committing some depredations, the clan was surrounded by a commando which had pursued them and succeeded in cutting them off among the rocks of a projecting shoulder of a great precipice. Here the retreating Bushmen turned for the last time at bay. Their untiring enemies were on one side, a yawning gulf without any chance of escape on the other. A dire but hopeless struggle for life commenced. One after another they fell under the storm of bullets with which their adversaries assailed them. The dead and dying were heaped upon the dizzy projecting ledge; many in their death struggle rolled and fell over among the crags and fissures in the depths which environed them. Still they resisted, and still they fell, until one only remained; and yet, with the bloody heap of dead around him and the mangled bodies of his comrades on the rocks below, he seemed as undaunted as when surrounded by the entire band of his brave companions. Posting himself on the very outermost point of the projecting rocks, with sheer precipices of nearly a couple of hundred feet on either side of him, a spot where no man would have dared to follow him, he defied his pursuers, and amid the bullets which showered around him he appeared to have a charmed life and plied his arrows with unerring aim whenever his enemies incautiously exposed themselves.

His last arrow was on the string. A slight feeling of compassion seemed at length to animate the hostile multitude that hemmed him in; they called to him that his life should be spared if he would surrender. He let fly his last arrow in scorn at the speaker, as he replied that "a chief knew how to die, but never to surrender to the race who had despoiled him!'' Then with a wild shout of bitter defiance he turned round, and leaping headlong into the deep abyss was dashed to pieces on the rocks beneath. Thus died, with a Spartan-like intrepidity, the last of the clan, and with his death his tribe ceased to exist.'

Two further quotations describe some of the final episodes. The Bloemfontein newspaper *The Friend* for 28th January 1854 recorded:

'Last week a party of burgers attacked a crowd of bushmen on the top of Thaba Pachoa mountain. [presumably Thaba Phatshwa near Ladybrand] Mr. Sefton and Mr. Strachan led the way. The commando was at the mountain at break of day, and just as the party was making its final arrangements the dogs began to bark, upon which a bushman came out to see what was the matter. He was shot dead. Immediately the fire of the attacking party became heavy, and the Bushmen replied with showers of poisoned arrows. At the end, it was found that nineteen persons, men, women, and children, had been killed. This sanguinary scene, dreadful though it may seem to some people at a distance, appears to us a terrible necessity. Eight of Mr. Sefton's horses and nineteen of Mr. van Tonder's oxen were found at the bushmen's kraal.'

And the diary of a lady traveller Mrs. Ralph Clarence for 19th April, 1867, when she was within a days journey of Pretoria coming from Natal, has this entry:[42]

'We are near Pretoria [at the Boshoffs]. The Boshoffs caught a family of eight Bushmen and kept them a year but now they have all run away.

About five years ago the farmers lost some cows and because they thought Bushmen had stolen them, they shot 400 Bushmen. Later the cattle were returned by Matopo [a Bantu chief] who said his people had stolen them.'

Let us hope the farmers were pulling the lady's leg, but it is to be feared that this story was true.

An incident somewhat similar to the massacre at Thaba Pachoa, related by J. M. Orpen[43], took place only the next year at Vaalbank Spruit eight miles south of Winburg. This time, however, there was a well meant but bungled attempt to parley before the shooting started and the losses were not all on the Bushman side. Three white men lost their lives and five were wounded before the surviving Bushmen made a fighting retreat northwards.

I have told elsewhere the story of the last organised band of the Bushmen of the Drakensberg and Maluti Mountains and how, fighting indomitably to the end under their chief Zweei, they were overcome and the chief killed in 1869, by combined Basuto and European action[34]. A few small bands lingered on in the Berg.

In 1878, Edith Kelly, an English girl newly arrived in South Africa, married a young farmer. They had an enviable ox-wagon honeymoon at Mont-aux-Sources (now the Royal Natal National Park) and in this lovely place encountered a party of Bushmen. 'Strange weird-looking creatures', commented the young bride 'hardly bigger than a child of ten', but she tells us little more[44]. Much may be forgiven a girl on her honeymoon in the way of ethnographical enquiry, but she missed a great opportunity for she was looking on the last band of the Drakensberg Bushmen.

F. C. Selous, famous hunter and pioneer, met Bushmen in the Waterberg District of the Transvaal in the '70s. By 1890 it is safe to say that, apart from the Lake Chrissie Bushmen only a few individuals remained in what is now the Republic of South Africa and these on sufferance on the farms.

During the whole long war only two serious attempts to come to terms with the Bushmen seem to have been made. In 1798 Lord Macartney, the Governor at the Cape, ordered the veldkornets on the north-eastern frontier to try to make peace by offering the Bushmen cows and sheep and promising periodical presents[2]. The offer was accepted and the animals freely given by the frontier farmers were handed over. The admirable attempt failed. The Bushman having no government only those who had personally made the agreement and accepted cattle considered themselves bound by it, others continued to raid the white men's farms and the Bushmen cattle-owners were themselves plundered by their wilder brethren living further inland.

Another attempt was made by the Colonial office in Natal in 1846 when a party was sent under J. Uys, with John Shepstone as interpreter, to offer the Bushmen in Griqualand East (then Faku's Country) a 'location' in which to settle down[34]. The Bushmen replied that they could live no other life than the one they had always lived. It is implicit in this reply and in their whole fierce and prolonged resistance to 'domestication' that they considered only the life of a hunter worth living. In Dryden's words:

> 'They led their wild desires to woods and caves,
> And thought that all but savages were slaves.'

It was a life which kept their bodies and senses at the highest pitch of fitness, satisfied their every instinct, and allowed them ample time to practise in beautiful surroundings almost all the arts. Before blaming the Bushman refusal to embrace civilisation, look around, reader, at average twentieth–century man – pot-bellied and purblind, bored and scowling, perpetually worried, lucky to have at considerable expense and for a few days only in the year what the Bushman had for nothing all the time – and say whether the little people had not at least, a case.

The progress of the war against the Bushmen is summarised on the map (Fig. 6), the product of much research. The frontiers are those between the *fighting* Bushmen and their enemies; a few Bushmen, responding to kind treatment, or because of capture, remained in the white occupied areas and some drifted back in their old age, when peace, for lack of men of fighting age, returned to the survivors.

It will be noticed that the settlers did not have it all their own way. The 1795 frontier is many miles to the south of the 1750 line in the region of the Roggeveld and Nieuwveld because of the retirement of the farmers from this area about 1754. The numbers on the map show places where historical encounters with Bushmen took place. These are a selection only from my notes for the preparation of the map and as they are mainly of local interest the references are given in a separate appendix.

This in brief is the history of a people who fought for their freedom to live in their own way until hardly an able-bodied man was left alive, and whose fighting qualities and fearlessness of death compelled the admiration of their bitter foes; yet who have been described by Mrs. Elizabeth Marshall Thomas as 'The Harmless People', submissive by nature, having it 'not in their nature to fight' and 'deploring and misunderstanding bravery': judgments hardly in accordance with their history![46] Hers is nevertheless a charming book full of observation and sympathy.

Many of the rock paintings record historical events. On the farm Beersheba in Griqualand East is an elaborate and spirited painting which tells its own story (see Plate 3). A mounted

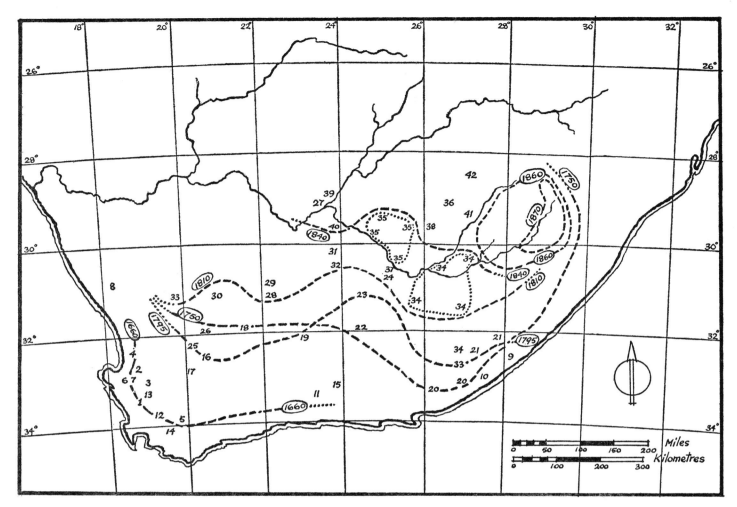

Fig. 6. The fighting retreat of the Bushmen. The numbers refer to notes in the Appendix, page 85.

commando has caught up with the Bushmen driving off stolen cattle. The farmers are firing from the saddle or dismounted and long streaks of smoke issue from their *roers*. Some Bushmen have already fallen, others fight back with their bows and arrows. The battle can only have resulted in defeat for the Bushmen but someone survived to paint this scene. The incident is not otherwise recorded but the date must be about 1850.

This was the direction in which Uys' and Shepstone's party had found Bushmen and another account, in the Natal Archives at Pietermaritzburg, shows that raids into Natal came often from this direction. It shows also that these Bushmen were still on good terms with the Bantu of the neighbourhood. As a little known historical document it is worth quoting in full:

'11th, June, 1856.

Statements of Untshali, Mgwai, Ngagule Zoboshigana, Ntsuku, Mhili and Solshe kase, of the Tribe of Lugajo sent with the others by direction of the Acting Govnr. to ascertain the position of the Bushmen who robbed the cattle of the Tribe of Lugajo.

We were sent by the Field Cornet Potgieter to trace up the spoor of the cattle taken from Lugajo last spring, there were three hundred and forty head taken on that occasion.

We followed the spoor accordingly and in doing so crossed Umkomanzi Umko-

24

many and Umzimkulu Ingnagimane, Umzinhlanga and Umzimvubu – the spoor went along under the Drakensberg and on the right hand of the Umzimkulu it took up the "White Drakensberg" (i.e. the minor but parallel range of those mountains) after continuing along its crest a distance which took us four days to travel over it turned down to the left and went in among a tribe of Diko (Amanpondo Inuse). We remained about in the mountains for two or three days endeavouring to ascertain the number and position of this tribe – we saw their kraals, and cattle feeding below, we also saw the people but none of them saw us.

We are quite sure that the spoor of this lot of cattle went in among this tribe for we traced them until we found ourselves quite among their kraals and were only not seen because of the haze and smoke in the atmosphere. We knew them to be the Amampondomyo because of the manner in which they built their kraals. They reside on the Umzimvuto high up at a place called the "Rode" where the spoor took us – it is from this beyond and above the Putsizma mountain.

Untshali one of the messengers sent, states that he was brought up in that country and knows it well, he describes this tribe as always having lived on terms of intimacy with the Bushmen with whom they intermarry and perpetuate the various forays for which they are remarkable. He describes the residence of these people to be of recent origin from the appearance of the huts and kraal.

Messengers further state that they counted two hundred and twenty head of cattle which the robbers had destroyed on the way.'

Other historical paintings occur on the farm Kwartelfontein on the Caledon River about 30 miles from its junction with the Orange River. They record what must have been one of the first ventures of Europeans into the district (see Plate 4). A letter from C. S. Orpen to Professor T. Rupert Jones of the Geological Society of London dated 18th March, 1885, describes these paintings which still clearly show Europeans with their muskets, powder horns hanging from their belts, and their horses. The knee-breeches which they wear, according to Orpen, point to the beginning of the nineteenth century at the latest and the farmers told them that the paintings were certainly there in 1835. He suggests that the people represented may have been members of Captain (later Colonel) Gordon's expedition who reached the 'Great River' (Orange) just south of this place in 1777[2]. They did not cross the river, however, so must have been painted from memory if it is their portraits on the rock. Orpen made a copy of the painting which is in the National Museum, Bloemfontein. The site was rediscovered by the present writer with the aid of Orpen's description.

4
Hunting and Fishing

In hunting antelope, his favourite quarry, the Bushman had somehow to get the animal within the short range of his weak bow, or use other means of killing. His ways of getting near enough to shoot were stalking, driving the game into ambush, and running down the animal.

In stalking he would sometimes, if in grass land, tie grass around his head so that he would be well camouflaged even when raising his head to observe his prey. More often, however, he would wear the skin and head of an animal – either the animals hunted or another which it did not fear – to deceive the game. Expertly miming the actions of the animal whose skin he wore and approaching not directly but by a spiral course he could approach close enough to loose his shaft. In tall grass a cap alone would be sufficient, like the springbok *be-creeping cap* seen by Burchell south of Prieska[47] (Plates 6, 7). The caps and the more elaborate disguises are commonly shown in the rock paintings.

An ostrich's feathers, neck and head were also commonly used in the manner shown in Stow's famous copy of a rock painting in the Herschel district of Cape Province[12]. The feathers were fixed to a light frame and a stick through the neck allowed the hunter to imitate the bird's natural actions of pecking, then lifting its head to swallow as he slowly advanced. Sir James Alexander found one of these contraptions still in use in South-West Africa[48] and Dornan describes its use by the Masarwa of Northern Bechuanaland[49].

Silayi, a native who lived with Bushmen in the mountains west of Pondoland, told how a sheepskin was similarly used when sheep-stealing[32].

A painting from Leeuwfontein, Wodehouse District shows not one but two hunters using an antelope's skin as a stalking disguise. In this practice by hunters long ago, we see, perhaps, the remote origin of the comic circus or pantomime horse, for the disguises were also used by dancers and actors for entertainment and probably for magic.

Ambushing was effected by driving the game to the point where the concealed archers crouched (Plate viii). This was easiest to do in a narrow defile from which the animals could not escape sideways, but in flat country more ingenious means were devised to keep them moving towards the trap. Antelope, like horses, will shy away from the unfamiliar thing, and it was found that they would not pass a line of ostrich feather tufts tied to sticks set in the ground. Fig. 7 shows how the feather brushes were arranged to bring buck to the place of ambush: it is adapted from a sketch made by a Bushman for Dr. W. H. J. Bleek[50].

Running down buck was done by relays of men keeping the animal continually on the move, no doubt in a wide circle if possible, until it would lie down, too exhausted to rise as the hunters closed in for the kill.

On the plains forming the Western part of the Bushman territory pitfalls were much used to trap the larger animals. Pits too deep for the victim to struggle out of were covered with

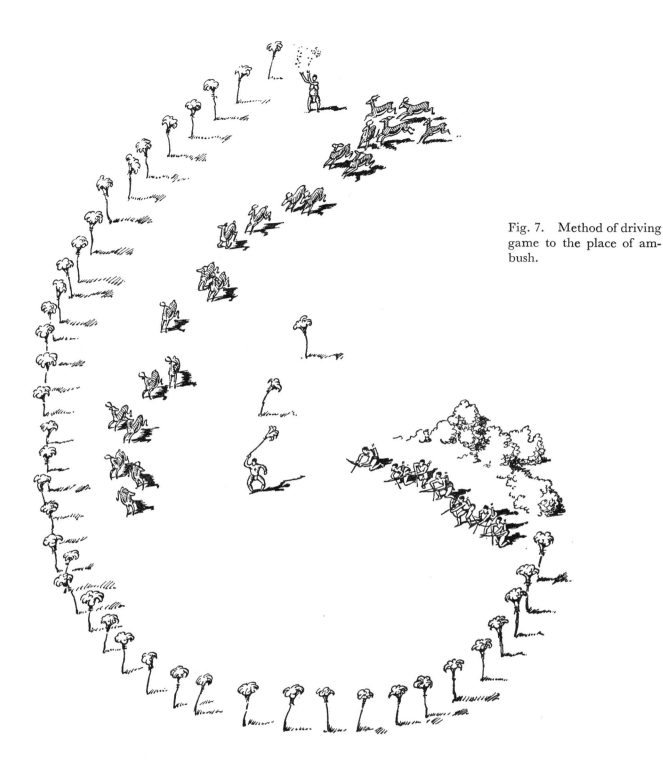

Fig. 7. Method of driving game to the place of ambush.

branches, grass, etc., and sometimes provided with sharp stakes to impale any beast which fell in. The methods of driving already described were employed to force animals in the direction of the pitfall. More elaborate means of contriving this were encountered by such travellers as Burchell and Galton[51] by which fences of stakes and branches as much as a mile or two in length would be arranged to form a funnel with the pitfalls at its end, into which game could be driven. Or whole valleys would be crossed by such a fence with a few gaps left through which the game must pass and which, of course, would have traps so placed that they could not be avoided.

One has looked in vain for evidence of such pitfalls in the eastern mountains. Probably the

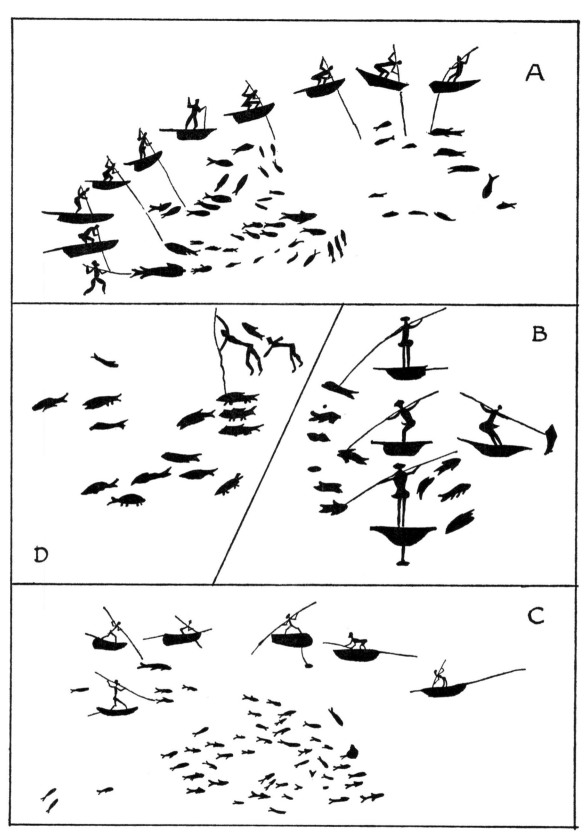

Fig. 8.   Harpooning fish.

A   Mpongweni mountain, Underberg, Natal. Harpooning from small boats or floats. After W. W. Battiss.
B   Kenegha Poort, Griqualand East.
C   Tsoelike River, Basutoland. After drawing by P. Vinnicombe its discoverer.
D   Uysberg, Ladybrand, O.F.S. Similar scene without the craft. After W. W. Battiss.

abundance of natural obstacles formed by lines of rocky cliffs and deep gorges, and the ease by which game could be killed by other means, made unnecessary the considerable labour of digging pits with only sharpened sticks as tools.

One has sought also in the rock paintings for scenes which might show another hunting method which was used by the palaeolithic hunters of Europe and until recently by Australian Aborigines and North American Indians. This was to drive the animals over a cliff and then dispatch those not killed outright. Mr. Harald Pager has brought to my notice a scene which bears just that interpretation. It occurs in a small shelter in a narrow gorge near Tynindini, Herschel district, a place eminently suitable for applying this method (Plate 8). A number of eland in the finest shaded polychrome technique are shown in various unnatural attitudes, some on their backs, some apparently with broken limbs, just as they would look if they had been driven over the krans opposite the shelter from which, as they lay shattered, the Bushmen artist recorded the scene. One of the animals is already being cut up.

There are traditions that Bushmen dug holes in which to hide and, having got in would pull a small bush or flat stone over the top, popping up to loose their arrows as an animal passed or was driven by [122]. It is probably this practice which gave rise to the legend of Bushmen being 'earth-men', living in holes in the ground.

Snaring small buck and other quadrupeds and birds, and poisoning water holes were other methods of procuring meat.

But the Bushmen were fishermen as well as hunters, using traps and harpoons expertly. Barrow found their fishing tackle, in good order and obviously recently used, in several places on the Orange River. The traps he says.[52]

> 'consisted of baskets made of osiers, and the stems of reeds alternately worked in: one being white, and the other dark-brown, gave them a very pretty appearance. The workmanship was firm and neat, and the contrivance sufficiently clever, being of the same nature as those wicker-baskets used in Europe for the like purpose. We found also several harpoons of wood, some pointed with bone, and fixed to ropes made apparently of some sort of grass.'

Alexander found similar baskets in use in the Fish River and he describes the method of use[48]. Some Bushmen would wade into the river, each having a basket between his legs with its mouth to the front, while other Bushmen also wading would drive the fish towards the baskets. Similar baskets are still used by the Lake Chrissie Bushmen and the Masarwa.

Stow also describes the harpoons and tells us how highly the barbed bone points were valued by their owners[31]. He mentions also that small fish were shot with arrows having a light line attached, and gives more details about the use of the fish baskets. Both he and Lichtenstein[35] describe the employment of fish weirs. These were used in two ways. One, analogous to the erecting of fences as above described, left only a few gaps for fish to pass at which points the baskets would be placed. The other way was to build enclosures against the banks by piling up stones as crude walls: when the stream rose after rain and fell again fish would be left trapped behind the walls while the water would run out between the stones. In principle these are the same as the tidal *vywers* or fish-traps found around the South African coast all the way from St. Helena Bay to Kosi Bay[54].

Even if we did not have historical records of the use by Bushmen of fish-spears we would still know of this from the rock paintings, five of which clearly show the fishermen thrusting at the swimming fish or lifting them from the water wriggling on the spear-point (Fig. 8)[21, 34, 55, 56, 57, 58] What is more surprising since it is not supported historically is that in three of the fishing scenes the harpooners are shown standing up in small canoes or coracles. No case is known of Africans, Bushmen or Bantu, using any such craft south of the Limpopo except in Moçambique, but the rock paintings are too clear to leave any doubt about what is represented. The figures are standing in rather than on the floating objects so these are apparently not floats. Some show a small bow-sprit, probably the end of a stick which stiffened the craft, which could have been made of sewn skins or matted reeds.

Whether fish baskets are also shown in the paintings is not so certain. Some designs which have been labelled 'schematic art' e.g. a painting at Tradouw Pass in the Western Cape[59], paintings shown in Stow's Plate 25[12] and others from Rhodesia[59] and many of the petroglyphs could be so interpreted. Mrs. P. Carter (née Vinnicombe) has recently published another from Bamboo Mountain near Himeville[60].

Two paintings are known, which seem to show two fishermen using a rod and line perhaps with a gorge (a short piece of bone or wood sharpened at both ends) in lieu of a hook. Such gorges are still used in Moçambique[118] and one was reported to have been found with a line made from a wild vine near the mouth of the Gouritz River in Cape Province in a hole close to a *vywer*[54].

5
Bushman Folklore

Most of what is known of the folk tales of the Bushmen we owe to the patient work of Dr. W. H. I. Bleek and his sister-in-law Miss Lucy Lloyd[50]. It was gathered mainly from 'Colonial' Bushmen, i.e. those living in what is now the Cape Province. A few more stories were recorded by J. M. Orpen from Bushmen in Basutoland[61]. To these sources the reader is referred, for the stories cannot be retold here except for those which give clues to the interpretation of the rock art and a few excerpts to illustrate their general character.

The latter is important for the insight it gives into the Bushman mind. It has been said of the countries of Europe that the best way to understand their peculiar national characters is to study their fairy tales. This is no doubt true of all peoples.

The Bushmen, it has already been pointed out, had a considerable fund of empirical knowledge of the world about them – of the behaviour of the heavenly bodies, the ways of the animals, the properties of the plants and minerals, the weather signs. But they had also a childlike desire to know the 'how' and the 'why' of things and it was from their pre-scientific attempts to explain the origins and workings of natural phenomena that much of their folk-lore arose. The result was often an odd mixture of sound observation, partially correct inference and absurdity.

The origin of the Bushmen themselves, described as the First Bushmen or the Men of the Early Race, was, according to one account, by coming out of a great hole in the ground – a kind of primal womb – followed by the animals. There is a kind of poetic truth in much of their folk-lore: do not all things come ultimately from the earth and are not men and animals of the same clay?

Typical of their poetic-scientific explanations of celestial phenomena is their reason for the waning and waxing of the moon as summarised by Dr. Bleek:

> 'The Moon is looked upon as a man who incurs the wrath of the Sun, and is consequently pierced by the knife (i.e. rays) of the latter. This process is repeated until almost the whole of the Moon is cut away, and only one little piece left; which the Moon piteously implores the Sun to spare for his (the Moon's) children. From this little piece, the Moon gradually grows again until it becomes a full moon, when the Sun's stabbing and cutting processes recommence.'

The phases of the moon are thus correctly seen to be caused by the sun, not as originating in the moon itself.

Illuminating also is the story of the Dawn's-Heart star which shows the remarkable acuity of Bushman vision as well as keenness of observation. The star was in fact the planet Jupiter, often a morning star, and the basic facts of the elaborate story are that the Dawn's-Heart is father to a daughter whom he swallows and after a while spits out again. This can hardly be other than their explanation of the disappearance of one of Jupiter's moons as it passes behind

Fig. 9. Leading the rain animal over the land. After J. M. Orpen. From Basutoland.

the planet in temporary occlusion and then reappears, but even Jupiter's brightest moon can be seen by very few, if any, people of other races without optical aid.

A solar eclipse was regarded as a natural phenomenon with hardly any mythological explanation. The origin of the milky way is pure fantasy, it is wood ashes thrown into the sky by a girl 'of the Early Race'.

The chief character in Bushman mythology, the praying mantis, had the name written in Dr. Bleek's orthography ! Kaggen. This begins with a dental click sound difficult for Europeans to pronounce, so I will call him Mantis. He is a creature of contradictory character, clever and stupid, kindly and cruel, brave and timid; in short he is human, a kind of dream Bushman, as Miss Dorothea Bleek put it. But he has supernatural powers which he has used to create the different kinds of antelope (also the moon, made from an old shoe), and which he loved to use also to play mischievous tricks on people, especially his ability to assume the form of any animal at will. His idea of a great joke, for example, was to take the form of a dead hartebeest in the path of some children out collecting veld food and allow them to cut up his body to take home. As they walk along heavily laden with the dismembered animal the head speaks, giving the children a terrible fright so that they drop the pieces and run, leaving the Mantis-hartebeest to re-assemble himself by his magic. The story is told with a wealth of circumstantial detail.

Mantis is married to the Dassie (the hyrax or rock-rabbit) and their children are the young Mantis, another son and daughter whose forms are not described, and an adopted daughter the Porcupine who married a mysterious being, Kwammanga, somehow identified with the rainbow. Of this union came young Kwammanga and the Ichneumon (a kind of mongoose) who is always arguing with Mantis, his grandfather. All this is dream stuff and the doings of this curious family filled many pages of Dr. Bleek's and Miss Lloyd's note-books.

In spite of his creative powers and ability to bring the dead to life again he was not worshipped by the Cape Bushmen though they prayed to the moon his creation. The Basutoland Bushmen however did seem to regard Mantis as a deity, creator and master of all things.

Who is this Kwammanga, of human shape yet seen in the rainbow? It is a poor archaeologist who never speculates so I will hazard a guess, remembering that although the Bushman's explanations were fanciful he was an accurate observer of celestial events. A Bushman out hunting early one morning climbs a hill. The mists of the night have risen to form a thin layer of stratus cloud which wreaths the hill-top. The climber passes through the cloud bank emerging suddenly as he reaches the top to find the sun still low at his back and before him a great wonder. On the silver cloud top a huge dark figure looms. Though distorted it has human form and it is framed by the brilliant colours of a rainbow. The figure is his shadow and the phenomenon 'the Brocken Spectre', but thus is a legend born.

Dr. Bleek's 'Colonial' Bushmen coming from the dry Great Karoo and the fringes of the Kalahari were much concerned with the observances necessary to rain making. The Rain or Water was a personage to be propitiated: if one angered Rain by killing frogs or otherwise

32

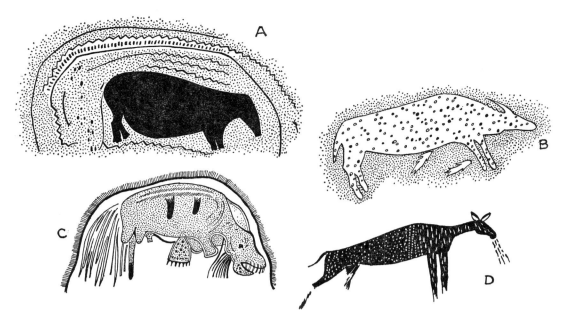

Fig. 10. *Rain animals* (see page 34).

A La Rochelle, Clarens, O.F.S. Animal under rainbow. After Miss J. R. Harding.

B Willow Grove, Wodehouse district, Cape Province. Spotted animal with fish. After H. Tongue.

C Klein Aasvogelkop, Rouxville, O.F.S. Spotted animal under rainbow. After G. W. Stow.

D Giant's Castle Game Reserve, Natal. Spotted animal, perhaps spitting forth rain.

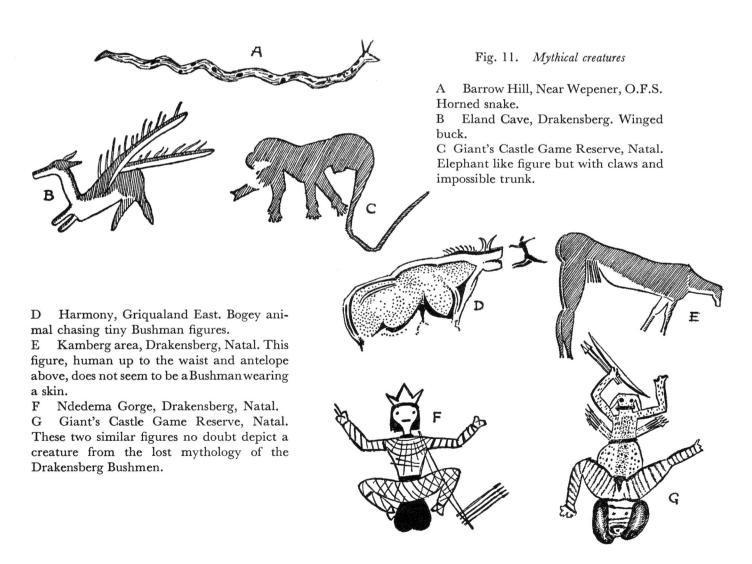

Fig. 11. *Mythical creatures*

A Barrow Hill, Near Wepener, O.F.S. Horned snake.
B Eland Cave, Drakensberg. Winged buck.
C Giant's Castle Game Reserve, Natal. Elephant like figure but with claws and impossible trunk.

D Harmony, Griqualand East. Bogey animal chasing tiny Bushman figures.
E Kamberg area, Drakensberg, Natal. This figure, human up to the waist and antelope above, does not seem to be a Bushman wearing a skin.
F Ndedema Gorge, Drakensberg, Natal.
G Giant's Castle Game Reserve, Natal. These two similar figures no doubt depict a creature from the lost mythology of the Drakensberg Bushmen.

33

interfering with Rain's things such as the water tortoise or a certain fungus, great storms might follow, and the guilty person might be carried off in a whirlwind or turned into a frog or snake. Rain was often thought of as an animal which lived in a pool. Wherever it walked on land rain would fall so the rain-doctors (this was their story) would lassoo the animal around its horns with a leather thong and drag it over the land (Fig. 9). This animal is represented in the rock paintings usually rather like an eland and often (like some South American rain-gods) spotted as though by the falling rain (Fig. 10).

It is clear from some of the accounts given to Dr. Bleek that the rain cloud itself was seen as the rain animal[63]. As the great dark cumulo-nimbus cloud moved across the sky overhead the Bushmen were looking up at the belly of a gigantic beast. Its legs were the separate columns of descending rain. If it was quiet and rained gently it was a Rain-cow; if it rained fiercely and with thunder it was a Rain-bull bellowing and the people took cover. Rain-cows were naturally preferred. One old rain-maker was requested:

> 'You must not arouse a Rain-bull, but you must make a She-rain, which is not angry, which rains gently, because it is a slow shower. It is one that falls gently, softening the ground, so that it may wet inside the earth. For people are afraid of a He-rain, when they hear it come thundering, as it gets its legs.'

The rain animal was ridden by dead men and it was to them the Bushmen addressed incantations if it seemed that the rain would pass them by.

> 'O gallopers
> O gallopers
> Do you not know me?
> You do not seem to know my hut.'

One is reminded that Jupiter in his character of the giver of rain, the thunderer, was portrayed riding upon a bull.

The animal came from the water and had to return to it again after rain had fallen where it trod: is not this also a practical expression of a scientific fact realised by the Bushmen, that the water-vapour which condenses into clouds does arise from the water and will eventually return to it to repeat the cycle? Shelley expressing the same idea made his cloud say:

> 'I am the daughter of Earth and Water,
> And the nursling of the sky:
> I pass through the pores of the ocean and shores;
> I change, but I cannot die.'

As we have seen, many of the folk-tales are explanations of natural phenomena. Others are cautionary tales to instruct the young, with grim accounts of what happened to children who were disobedient or who neglected one of the many observances necessary to ward off ill-fortune. The terrible bogey-animals among the paintings, often shown chasing little Bushman figures, probably illustrated some of these tales. There was also a monstrous horned serpent some 20 or 30 feet in length which could crush a full grown hartebeest. This snake is fairly commonly shown in the paintings and represents a wide-spread belief, for the animal-headed snake, sometimes with horns and sometimes without, occurs in the rock paintings of Rhodesia and South-West Africa as well as in the Republic of South Africa (Fig. 11).

Other stories again seem to have no educational or moral purpose but are told merely to entertain, such as the amusing story of the All-Devourer, apparently a human but of prodigious appetite. Mantis and his family make the mistake of inviting him to dine, sending a

6. Giant's Castle Game Reserve, Drakensberg, Natal. Hunters wearing antelope head masks. Hanging down their backs are what look like thongs or cords with knobs at their ends. Could these be bolas? These weapons are not known to have been used in Later Stone Age times and only one other known painting could bear this interpretation. The standing figure is about 7 inches high.

7. Giant's Castle Game Reserve. Two hunters in polychrome wearing antelope head masks. The leading figure carries two small buck. Underlying are earlier paintings of hartebeeste and to the left one of the controversial cloaked figures of the Drakensberg. The latter hunter is about 13 inches high.

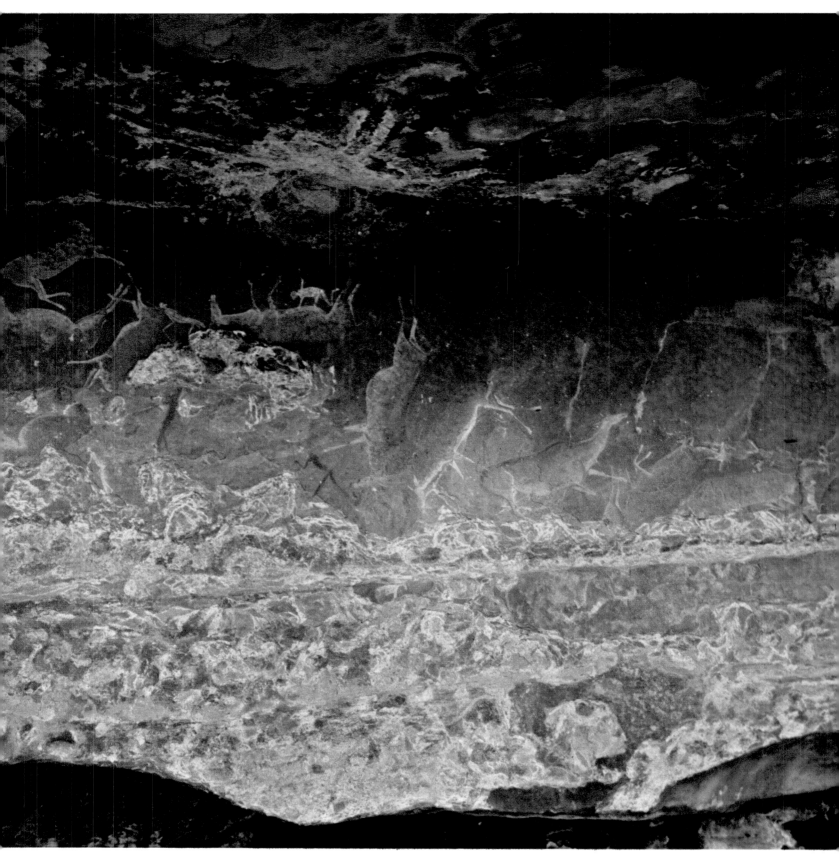

8. Tynindini, Herschel district. Elands in beautiful shaded polychrome in attitudes suggesting that they have fallen over the krans opposite the shelter. (See page 29)

9. Wright's Shelter, Kamberg area, Drakensberg, Natal. Mythical creature, half man half mantis. About 5 inches long.

10. Same site as last. Two grazing rhebokke, the one on the left in foreshortened front view. The animal on the right is about 3 inches long.

11. Ezelzacht near Oudtshoorn, Cape Province. Figures fish-like up to the waist and human above, reminiscent of the mer-people of European folklore and perhaps having the same origin. (See page 35). The whole group is about 15 inches across.

bag of cooked meats as hors d'oeuvres. They see him coming by the disappearance of the bushes in his path as he gulps them down. He arrives and after more hors d'oeuvres is given a bucket of soup which he swallows bucket and all. More buckets of meat, a few bushes, the Mantis's house and all the Mantis's sheep go the same way. Then the awkward guest asks where is the food he was invited to eat. On being told he has had it he angrily devours the Mantis himself, then Kwammanga with the bed on which he happened to be sitting. But the young Mantis and the young Kwammanga attacking together cut the All-devourer's stomach on both sides and out pour their fathers, the sheep, the buckets and all.

Their folklore does not disclose any very definite beliefs in a life after death though, as we have seen, dead men rode the Rain, and Stow was told vaguely of a place to which dead Bushmen go. The moon also when hollow in its first quarter is carrying people who are dead. Another story seems to accept the finality of death but implies that it was not always so. Once a young person was weeping for his mother who had just died. And the Moon spoke to comfort him saying that his mother 'was not altogether dead' but would return again alive. This the son refused to believe and the Moon was very angry for was not he (the Moon was male) himself the proof of his assertion, dying and coming to life once a month. He struck the boy, breaking his lip and turned him into a hare to bear the cleft lip for ever; and he cursed the people that when they died there should be no returning.

In contrast with the 'fairy' tales of Europe, many of which are brutal and sadistic, Bushman folklore does not glorify violence or cruelty. Its heroes are not the strong but the little people who gain their ends by patience and cleverness – the hyena, the mongoose, the Mantis himself. Sexual adventure is hardly ever the theme of a story and pornography had no place either in their tales or in their art.

Their many tales of transformation of humans into beasts or birds and vice versa show how clearly they identified themselves with the animal kingdom. The long periods spent observing and imitating the animals they stalked seem to have given them a kind of empathy which is perhaps the secret of the liveliness of their animal paintings. The artist as he painted the galloping buck or playful baboon *was* that animal and knew not only its every action but even how it felt.

The story behind the paintings in Plate 11 was, according to Dr Bleek, told to a Mr Ballot by an old Bushman then still living in the district, but this record seems to have been lost[113]. It is described as a fine old legend, the subject being the 'watermaidens'. The site is only about 30 miles from the sea and we can plausibly guess that the creatures, fish-like up to the waist and human above, were based upon the marine mammal the dugong of the Indian Ocean seen by Bushmen at the coast. This animal or its near relation the manatee is believed also to have given rise to the mermaid legend of European folklore.

It is unfortunate that there was no Bleek or Orpen on the Natal side of the Drakensberg to record the myths of the area richest in rock art. We can never know the story illustrated by the Pegasus-like winged buck of the great Eland Cave, or who are the creatures – half human and half animal, yet armed with bows and arrows – from the N'dedema Gorge and Giant's Castle. Many such strange creatures must remain unidentified and many scenes baffle interpretation (Fig. 11).

6

The Art – Descriptive Terms, Materials, Techniques and Distribution

The study of prehistoric art in South Africa has formed something of a no-man's-land between the archaeologists and the art-historians, and has therefore been much neglected. The dual aspect of a painting as an artefact to the scientist and a work of art to the critic has prevented the emergence of a generally accepted system of description and classification, for it was often the indefinable qualities which the archaeologist, as such, must ignore, which were the most important to the art critic; 'the peculiar function of art begins where the powers of language end'.[64] Scientists do not like imponderables, artists do not like to limit themselves to the verbally definable; the result has been an unhappy mixture of objective scientific and sub-jective art jargon, so that we find no less eminent a man than the Abbé Breuil using such descriptions as 'black figures of fine style' and 'degenerate polychromes' or even 'good art'.[65, 66]

Though I fully sympathise with the art critic's point of view about the limitations of language in describing works of art, it seems to me more reasonable to use language only as far as it *is* definable and beyond that point to let the work of art speak for itself.

Most of the terms used are simple enough to define. A colour is any which the normal eye can clearly distinguish, light and dark red for example being different colours, and black and white being also colours. Monochrome, bi-chrome and polychrome respectively describe a painting done in one, two, and more than two 'colours'. 'Shading' is the gradual and deliberate merging of one colour into another to avoid a sharp division between them, and 'modelling' is a special case in which shading is used to give the appearance of solidity to a painting on a more or less flat surface. Since shading involves the use of two colours plus a third produced by the mixing all shaded paintings are polychromes. 'Shadowing' is another way of giving a three dimensional look to a painting by using a darker tint without shading.

Terms descriptive of aspect such as front and rear view, and lateral view or profile, need no definition but the use of 'silhouette' as a synonym for profile is incorrect. Strictly speaking a silhouette is a representation in one colour and in any aspect without a drawn outline, like the shadow which originally gave M. de Silhouette the idea, but the term can be stretched to include cases with a faint outline. It follows that all monochromes are silhouettes as well as vice versa. A profile may or may not be a silhouette.

To 'foreshorten' means, according the Oxford Dictionary, 'to delineate so as to cause to be apparently shortened in the direction not lying in a plane perpendicular to the line of sight'. This definition seems to exclude views (of an animal for instance) directly from the front or rear.

It is when we come to terms descriptive of manner or style that watertight definitiou

36

becomes difficult, if not impossible. What is 'style' itself? One can only say that it is the sum total of the characteristics of an artist's work and since no two artists paint in precisely the same way there are in a sense as many 'styles' as there are artists. But this is only stating the philosophic truth that all things are unique, and in order to think at all about art some grouping is necessary. Whether two paintings are sufficiently alike to be considered of the same style must, however, remain to some extent a matter of subjective judgment.

All systems of classification run into difficulties with border-line cases but graphic and glyptic art can be classified in the first place as representational or non-representational. The former, with which we are chiefly concerned in this study, can in theory range from the completely 'naturalistic' by graduations of 'abstraction' to the 'schematic', terms it is better to illustrate rather than attempt to define. Completely naturalistic paintings (i.e. a photographic likeness) do not occur in Bushman art (if they exist at all), for the artist's mind selects (i.e. abstracts) for stressing certain elements in what he sees, but the paintings of animals are to a large extent naturalistic. Abstraction necessarily involves leaving out and this can be carried to the extreme of, for example, depicting an animal by only the line of its back with two lines as legs and one horn. The Bushmen did not in fact produce such 'schematic' work, but some of their paintings of human figures come near to this style. Naturalistic paintings of humans were not done either; heads, for example, were usually just blobs, and the bodies, though not quite schematic, were reduced to a very simple form. This degree of abstraction is usually referred to as conventionalisation. Female figures are shown in more bodily detail but the heads remain featureless.

The reason for this difference in the manner of depicting animals (more or less naturalistic) and human beings (more or less conventionalised) was discussed in *Rock Paintings of the Drakensberg*. The conventionalised (partially schematic) human figures are almost always shown in action and it would be sufficient explanation of their simplicity to say that it was only the action, not the form, which the artist wished to depict. This I think is true and it is noteworthy that when animals are shown in rapid movement they too tend to be less naturalistically portrayed, but the theory fails to explain the complete absence of anything like a portrait of a human being and it was suggested that there was a tabu (surviving from the days of sympathetic magic but with its origin no doubt long forgotten) on naturalistic representation of the human figure.

One more term must be considered. 'Geometrical', a term applied to a few paintings and many petroglyphs, is also difficult to define. Apparently non-representational designs of circles, lines radiating from a point, parallel wavy lines, and similar forms can certainly be so described but many of the designs take no form easily describable in geometrical terms and do not represent anything recognisable either. For these neither geometrical nor schematic is the word. Symbol will not do either as they may not mean anything. The non-committal 'formling' has been used and seems the only word, unless we coin one such as 'cryptomorph'.

So much for description. The next stage of scientific study is of course classification and this can be usefully done only with a view to serving a specific purpose or purposes. One of the objects of the study (among many others) is to record and map the geographical distribution of the different types of painting or petroglyph, as this, considered in relation to the distribution of the stone industries and other data, may give clues to the migration of Stone Age peoples or the direction of diffusion of their cultures. Another aim is to determine from a study of the cases of superposition the chronological order of first occurrence of the different types of painting and to discover the boundaries within which such sequences hold good.

Paintings can be classified according to colour or colours, according to the *number* of colours, or subject, size, style, technique, etc., or some combination of these characteristics. Which to choose as the basis of classification can be decided only by trial to see which gives consistent results. Usefulness is the only test.

A simple classification by colour has not proved helpful to the study of distribution or relative age, since the same colours were used in different areas and at different periods. No more useful was an attempt to establish a sequence based on size alone, since the dimensions of the rock 'canvas' were obviously often the limiting factor. Some workers have suggested that paintings of different animals belong to different periods – a period of the rhebok, of the gazelle, and so on. This I find contradicted by the evidence as well as being intrinsically most unlikely.

Classification by number of colours (monochrome, etc.) has permitted some useful generalisations to be made, and the technique of shading has proved a valuable criterion, enabling shaded paintings to be dated within certain limits[67].

The working out of sequences of types of painting is an extraordinarily complex task. Since the paintings are infinitely variable, decisions largely subjective must continually be made as to whether two paintings belong in the same category, or not. An example was given in *Rock Paintings of the Drakensberg*.

The discovery of a pigment giving a new colour, or the art of shading, or any such new development did not of course necessarily result in the abandonment of the older ways, which continued to be followed at least by some artists. All that can be established therefore is the order of the *first* appearance of any kind of painting in a particular area. You may find that a sequence based on, say, colour and number of colours, carefully built up by much labour, is wrecked by a case of clear reversal, but you may then find that by taking another factor into account (such as size) or leaving one out, the sequence is preserved.

A great deal of work remains to be done in this field which could well be done by amateurs in their own areas. The position with regard to the Drakensberg paintings remains as outlined in *Rock Paintings of the Drakensberg* and may be summarised as follows:

In spite of the continuance of old ways of painting side by side with new, and of regressions and anticipations, careful study of the cases of super-impositions, observation of the *apparent* relative ages (i.e. the present clarity) of paintings subjected to the same conditions of exposure or protection, and study of the examples which can be dated by their subject, does disclose an evolution from simple to progressively more complex styles. Monochromes, bichromes, unshaded polychromes, and shaded polychromes appear in that order and this evolution was accompanied by increasing skill in the depiction of movement, in composition and in the portrayal of animal attitudes other than the lateral view, so that during the period of the shaded polychromes (approximately 1650–1860 AD.) the most difficult foreshortened attitudes were attempted with complete success. 'Modelling' as well as simple shading was at this time also brought to perfection.

The last few decades of rock painting in the Republic saw in most areas a regression to simpler styles. In examples certainly of this period there is no foreshortening and among the numerous polychromes of cattle shading occurs at only one site. This was the period in which the artists were fighting their final battles – the *mobilisation générale* as the Abbé Breuil has called it – and in such circumstances some decline of art is to be expected. The genius of some artists, however, rose superior even to these conditions and some fine representations of horses and horsemen appear among the last of the paintings. The experiments in perspective and representation in depth which were being made in the final period of the art will be referred to in a later chapter. So also will be the sequence of types of the petroglyphs.

Regarding the composition of the paints there seems no mystery about the pigments. These were various ochreous earths, ground up mineral oxides and coloured stone, and a powder found in concretions in the cave sandstone. Manganese and carbon provided blacks. Bird droppings, certain rubbery plant saps and possibly zinc oxide gave whites.

The media with which the pigments were mixed to make the paints are less certain. There are traditions that animal fats, bone marrow, and plant saps were so used. Other suggestions have been egg white, milk, honey, and urine[34]. A Basuto who learnt to paint from the Bushmen used ox blood as one constituent of his paint[115]. His paintings incidentally were greatly inferior to those of his tutors.

Mr. R. (Ginger) Townley Johnson, who with his friends Percy Sieff and Hymie Rabinowitz has found and recorded so many of the rock paintings of the Western Cape, carried out a valuable series of experiments to test the various suggested media, applying the paints to the Table Mountain sandstone on which in that region the paintings are found[68]. Mutton fat and marrow fat mixed well with the pigments and could be easily applied but fine lines were difficult to paint and some colours threw a halation on the sandstone which is hardly at all absorbent. On cave sandstone this would probably not happen. The plant juices mixed badly and it was impossible to make fine lines and sharp outlines with the paint. Gall was more successful but it would be difficult to obtain in sufficient quantity. Hyrax urine (a viscous liquid) could not be tried for lack of a cooperative specimen. Blood and milk it seems were not tried either. Honey was a complete failure. Only with egg tempera could Mr. Johnson make lines as fine as some in the Bushman paintings and this paint mixed and flowed well, and was insoluble in water. Bird's eggs, including those of the ostrich, would be easy enough to obtain.

It is likely that the Bushmen used many different media depending on what was locally available. It is probable also that they knew how to remedy a defect in one medium by mixing in a proportion of another.

The methods of application were apparently also various. Two independent eye-witness accounts report that brushes were used made from stiff hair such as that of the wildebeest's mane or tail[32, 69]. Another eye witness describes the use of bone spatulas[7] and Basuto traditions mention small feathers as brushes[9, 115].

It is clear from many unfinished paintings that in the case of bichromes and polychromes when one colour was white this was applied first and left exposed where required and it is quite possible that this was also done in the case of monochromes in red or other colours, as a primer to reduce suction on absorbent rock.

The rough distribution of the rock art was described in Chapter 1 (and see Fig. 2), but having now defined our terms, we can describe the art in more detail to note the ways in which the paintings differ in each zone and what is common to two or more. The petroglyphs of zone 4 are considered in detail in Chapter 9. It is necessary also to refer briefly to the art of Southern Rhodesia and South-West Africa. The characteristics of the different zones can be summarised as follows:

> zone 1: This is regarded as an extension of the Southern Rhodesian art zone into the Republic of South Africa. The paintings are mainly monochromes but there are a few bichromes and unshaded polychromes and one instance of shaded polychromes. The animals are represented in profile: there are no known examples of foreshortening. Scenes are few. Imprints of hands occur. Except for some cup-like markings and engravings of animal spoor there are no petroglyphs*. These engraved spoor occur also in Rhodesia, South-West Africa and (as we shall see) in zone 4. Rhodesia has also some petroglyphs of a geometrical and schematic nature but only one known naturalistic glyph of the kind found in zone 4.

> zone 2: In addition to simple monochromes, bichromes and unshaded polychromes similar to those of zone 1, there are also beautifully shaded polychromes often in foreshortened aspects. These are among the later paintings. Scenes of fighting, dancing, hunting, etc. are common. There are no hand imprints. The later paintings are considerably more detailed than those of the other two zones of the paintings.

> zone 3: The paintings resemble those of zone 1, but the work as a whole is cruder with fewer bichromes and polychromes. There is no shading or foreshortening. Imprints of hands are common. Scenes are few.

> zone 4: The petroglyphs of this zone are classified and described in Chapter 9.

As already noted there is, in all areas, a basic difference in the ways animals and human figures are depicted, the former being more or less naturalistic, the latter, especially the male figures, conventionalised. In all areas also action is skilfully shown but best in zone 2. The subjects are nearly always humans and animals. Plant life – fairly common in the paintings of Rhodesia – is very rare in the Republic and attempts at depicting scenery are almost unknown. Geometrical forms are also very rare in the paintings but commoner, as we shall see, in the petroglyphs, as also are plant forms.

The paintings of zone 3 closely resemble those of South-West Africa except that the latter region has more bichromes and has also a few polychromes, mainly in the Brandberg. The northern boundary of zone 3 is therefore quite arbitrary. Petroglyphs are common in South West Africa (see Chapter 1) but have not been found to extend into zone 3 south of the Orange River.

Of special interest are the hand imprints made by covering the front of the hand with paint and pressing it against the rock[70]. This is the expression of an almost universal impulse among rock painters to record as a sort of signature the hand of the artist. Such imprints are found in South-West Africa, everywhere in Central and North Africa where rock paintings occur, in Spain and France, in Australia, and in both North and South America. It is all the more curious therefore that, although they occur also in our zones 1 and 3, they are absent in zone 2 which contains about 70 per cent of the paintings of the Republic. I shall have more to say about the hand imprints in later chapters.

* Since the above was written I have discovered petroglyphs, painted and unpainted, in a Cave Sandstone rock shelter in the Limpopo Valley [119].

7

The Hottentots, the Foreigners and the Sea-beasts

'The very nerves and sinews of knowledge consist
in believing nothing rashly.'

Epicharmus (circa 500 B.C.)

A glance at the maps in Figs. 2, 3 and 5 reveals a striking triple correspondence between (a) the rock paintings of zone 3, (b) the distribution of Wilton artefacts in the Cape, and (c) the territory occupied by Hottentots in the latter half of the seventeenth century. This has led Mr. Jalmar Rudner, of Cape Town, to infer that the Hottentots were the bearers of the Wilton Culture of the Cape when they (as is generally agreed) migrated there from South-West Africa, and that they were the authors of *all* the rock paintings of zone 3[71, 72, 73].

Now the people called Hottentots by the European settlers were, as we have seen, a pastoral people owning large herds of cattle and sheep, and living in portable mat huts. As there are no representations of cattle and only a few of sheep in the rock paintings of the Southern and Western Cape Mr. Rudner has postulated a pre-pastoral hunter Hottentot people who occupied the same territory and presumably lived in rock shelters. This, however, is a contradiction in terms for it is clear from Van Riebeeck's[74] journals and other records and from the researches of physical anthropologists such as Professor P. V. Tobias[75] that the Cape Hottentots were a heterogeneous people varying considerably in stature and skull form. 'Hottentot' therefore has little or no meaning as describing a physical type and should only be used as a cultural term applicable to people living in the same way as the historical Hottentots to whom the name was originally given.

The elements of Hottentot culture by which it was distinguished from Bushman culture, e.g. the keeping of cattle and sheep and moving as the grazing needs of these animals demanded, and the art of making pottery, were certainly of northern origin and may well have been brought to South Africa by one of the physical types found among the Hottentots, who then intermarried with, and passed on their culture to, other people already here. The bearers of the pastoral Hottentot culture may have been, as Tobias has suggested, the people whose graves have been found along the Orange River near Kakamas although these graves cannot be dated on archaeological grounds.

Thus it is reasonable to rephrase Mr. Rudner's question to ask: were the zone 3 rock paintings the work of non-pastoral people other than the historical Bushmen? This is theoretically possible as there were certainly other types of Later Stone Age men in that region and some of them possessed the material elements of the Wilton culture. Such were the people, taller and otherwise physically different from the Bushmen whose remains have been found at Matjes River[76], at Oakhurst[77] and at Zitzikama[78], and in some of these cases the skeletons had interred with them grave stones bearing paintings similar to the rock paintings. It is therefore feasible that they should have been rock-painters also, although no paintings were found on the wall of the shelters in which the burials were found. So far I can go along with Mr Rudner though we cannot call these hunters and food gatherers 'Hottentots'. It is common ground also that most, at least, of the rock paintings of zone 3 were 'Wilton' art, and that Hottentots and objects of their culture are represented in rock paintings as were Bantu and European when the Bushmen were in contact with them. But Mr Rudner goes further and wishes to deny to the Bushmen the authorship of *any* of the rock paintings of this region, and this will not do at all. Bushmen were certainly possessors of the Wilton material culture, whoever else may have shared it with them, and they were also probably the sole makers of the almost indistinguishable Smithfield C stone implements[23], the distribution of which along the south coast is largely co-extensive with the Wilton material. Implements of this culture are also found in immediate association with rock paintings in zone 3 *and* in the other painting zones where Hottentots, however defined, are never known to have lived[79]. Moreover Bushmen were encountered by the early explorers in every part of the Southern and Western Cape which make up zone 3. That the Bushmen were the artists in zones 1 and 2 is an archaeological and historical certainty. That they should have refrained from painting in zone 3 is an entirely unnecessary assumption.

It remains however a theoretical possibility that some of the art was the work of people other than the historical Bushmen and this is one of the reasons why, in an archaeological tour of the Cape, I sought out rock shelters having painted hand imprints, which I then measured[70]. Statistical comparison of their sizes with the recorded hand sizes of Bushmen and Hottentots shows that the hand imprints were those of the former people or another of about the same stature. People as tall as the historical Hottentot were definitely excluded. The hand imprints occur in superpositions both under and over other paintings and are usually of the same colour as other paintings in the same shelter: it is fair to assume therefore that the imprints were those of the artists.

One other question is incidentally raised. The Hottentots of the Cape Peninsula and a considerable distance to the east seem not to have used metals until after the establishment of the Dutch station in 1652, although the Namaqua to the north had copper and iron and the Gonaqua to the east used iron. The use of iron in both cases was no doubt learnt from the neighbouring Bantu. Those Hottentots who had no metals must surely have used stone cutting implements. What type were they? Again the only answer can be Wilton tools, for these and, much more rarely, Smithfield C are the only Later Stone Age industries found in the area.

Another highly intriguing question is whether any foreign people are depicted in the paintings other than Europeans of the last three centuries, 'foreigners' being defined as coming from outside sub-Saharan Africa. That travellers from civilised lands might in ancient times have penetrated Southern Africa to be observed by the keen eyes of Bushmen or other hypothetical rock artists and their likenesses painted on the rock, is a seductive idea which has appealed to the imaginations of some distinguished scientists.

In *Rock Paintings of the Drakensberg* I discussed the examples of cloaked figures among rock paintings in the Berg which had been thought to represent Phoenicians and Arabs and showed that they were wearing the typical skin kaross which the Bantu certainly wore in that neighbourhood until they adopted the wearing of a blanket in lieu of a kaross after about 1830.

viii. Bushmen have driven a herd of various game, including the now extinct quagga, into a narrowing *kloof*, where they are under attack from Bushman arrows. One antelope lies stricken and a quagga rears as an arrow strikes. Already the vultures gather. An oil painting by Thomas Baines in the Africana Museum.

ix. Photograph of a copy of a painting from the Natal National Park, Mont-aux-Sources. Bushmen return from a successful hunt, the leading figure carrying a small buck. They wear short buck-skin karosses.

x. Frieze of paintings from Game Pass, Kamberg area, Drakensberg, Natal. Cloaked human figures, thought by some to represent Phoenicians, underlie and overlie shaded polychrome eland. The frieze as shown is about 10 feet long.

xi. Reinhart Maack's original sketch of the figure, later dubbed by the Abbé Breuil, the 'White Lady'. See also Plate 25 and discussion in text.

xii. Paintings from the Kranses, Kamberg area, Drakensberg. Eland, running Bushman figures and, to the left, a procession of Bantu. The whole group as shown is about 7 feet long.

xiii. Ikanti Mountain, near Sani Pass, Drakensberg. Numerous Bushmen, all males, on trek. The figures average 5 inches high.

xiv. Zuurfontein near Molteno, Cape Province. Polychrome ostriches. The birds are about 6 inches high.

xv. Martinshoek near Thodes, Cape Province. Eland being hunted by men and dogs. Below them are two small buck. The top eland is about 9 inches long.

The alleged foreigners in other parts of the country were beyond the scope of that book but shall receive full consideration here.

The missionary Albert Schweiger seems to have been the originator of the idea[80, 81]. In rock shelters in the valley of the Great Kei River Herr Schweiger found paintings which he decided represented Phoenician or Arabic sailors, Egyptian soldiers and a white queen (shades of the White Lady!). Always preferring the far-fetched identification to the simple he compared others to a Bedouin of the Sahara, an Australian native, a Persian priest, and a prehistoric reptile. His ideas were published in the *Catholic Magazine* in 1912 but not surprisingly were not taken seriously. The idea gained some respectability however when espoused by Professor Raymond Dart in a paper in *Nature* in 1925[82], in which he accepted some of the figures as being foreigners wearing Babylonian, Phrygian and Chinese caps. The Bushmen wore skin caps of various shapes and the 'Babylonian' cap worn by one figure is in my opinion one of these made from a cat's or monkey's skin with the tail left on. Professor Dart was also the first to suggest that certain paintings at Game Pass in the Drakensberg near Rosetta published as a black-and-white photograph in the *Natal Railway Guide* in 1903, were 'cloaked Asiatics of the Babylonic-Phoenician period' (Plate x). This interpretation was later accepted by the Abbé Breuil.

Of these paintings it is sufficient to say that some of the cloaked figures are painted *over* a shaded polychrome eland which can be dated to within the last three centuries[67, 83]. Even were this not so the paintings are extraordinarily clear and fresh and could not possibly be 2,500 years old as the Phoenician theory would require.

In articles in the *Illustrated London News* (1933) and the *Official Year Book of the Union of South Africa* (1936) the late Professor C. van Riet Lowe gave cautious and qualified support to Professor Dart in his interpretations, agreeing that foreigners were represented but not committing himself as to whether they were Phrygians, Babylonians, Egyptians, or others.

The Abbé Breuil, even before he commenced his work in Southern Africa, had accepted the idea and had identified as foreigners many figures in copies and photographs of rock paintings in South Africa, South-West Africa and Rhodesia. It is historically interesting to note that it was from black and white photographs that the Abbé first conceived his theory of the 'White Lady' (Plate 25), which figure he thus described:[84]

> 'These photographs revealed that the main figure was that of a young woman with typically Mediterranean, perhaps Cretan, profile.
> She is dressed in a clinging garment with a belt ornamented with four rows of pearls. Pearls also decorate her arms, knees, shoulders and breast, while a band of pearls stretches from her ear to her forehead and others again adorn her hair and hang round her neck. Her flesh is white and her hair dark reddish-brown, not quite reaching her shoulders, but cut squarely. A white stain partly hides the high forehead and continues down the long nose. The mouth is delicate and slightly opened and the lips are finely drawn. The chin is hidden in a cloth reaching to the ear. There can be no doubt about the Mediterranean character of the profile.'

In fairness to the Abbé Breuil it must be supposed that 'pearl' was a mistranslation of *perle* which can equally mean bead. No-one could claim to identify as pearls the minute dots in the painting.

The figure fascinated him before and after he saw it in the Brandberg cave and he described 'her' as of serene and magical beauty, supple and young. And it is indeed a charming figure, balanced, delicate and graceful.

On what did the Abbé's identification of this now famous painting depend? Why 'white' and why 'lady'? The body of the figure is pinkish to above the waist and dark above, with bands speckled as if beaded around the body and limbs. In the hair are perhaps other bands of beads. In one hand there is an object like a flower or cup, in the other a bow with an arrow nocked to the string and more arrows held against the bow-staff. The figure is about fifteen inches tall and appears to be wearing very brief shorts. It is a well known fact that in most rock art and certainly in that of Southern Africa the colour of the painting is rarely that of the object represented, an elephant is more likely to be red than grey, a baboon or a Bushwoman, digging stick and all, may be in white. The colour of the lower part of the figure therefore does not necessarily correspond with the skin colour of the person the artist was here depicting and even if it did could well represent body paint. So could the shorts the figure seems to wear. So the 'white' can be deleted from her title.

It should be made clear before going further that the paintings of the Maack Shelter are on rather rough and speckled granite. The Abbé's copies are reproduced in his books without any attempt to indicate the texture, colours, or pattern of speckling of the rock 'canvas'. This is no fault of his; it would no doubt be impossible by the techniques used. The unfortunate result however is that the copies simply do not look like the paintings and they give the impression of a clarity of outline and detail which the originals do not, and could not, have. An attempt to remedy this by the inclusion of black and white photographs is only partly successful; the paintings are not very photogenic. I have studied the figure *in situ* with a group of archaeologists and the general opinion, coinciding with mine, was that the face was not painted at all but was suggested by natural markings of the rock. But in any case to try to identify the race of the figure from a profile done on rough rock to this scale would be hazardous in the extreme; and almost every type of human profile can be found among the Bantu (Ovambo and Herero) of South-West Africa.

The head is in profile and the shoulders and torso are turned so as to be almost a full view, but it is not very clear whether we are seeing the 'lady's' back or front and this is of some importance in judging the sex. A little experiment (which, reader, please try, remembering that the bow is behind the rear leg) shows that the figure must have the left leg and left arm forward and the back towards us; any other attitude is impossibly twisted. The left breast would still be seen if it were there but the Abbé does not base his opinion of the figure's sex on the breasts which he says 'are not more marked than those of the person following her', which is unquestionably male. The page-boy hair style is shared by several male figures in the shelter so this is no indication of female sex. What remains? The delicacy of the figure? It seems to me that these thin thighs and small buttocks are rather those of a youth than of a woman. In the absence of any definite indication of sex it is infinitely more likely that any figure holding a bow in Africa (or even in Crete or Egypt) should be a man. And is there no indication?

Many paintings in all the painting zones of Southern Africa show the male organ with a line or bar across it near the end. What this means is not certain. The Abbé has referred to it as infibulation though male infibulation is unknown in Africa and is extremely rare elsewhere.

Fig. 12 (left). Makhetas, Basutoland. The cloaked figure shown in Plate 26, with small human figure superimposed. Note the quiver.

Fig. 13 (right). Makhetas. Note the similar quiver and the typical Bushman kaross.

In correspondence with the present writer he has expressed the opinion that it may be symbolic 'a graphic representation of a moral prohibition' i.e. against sexual intercourse, which was in primitive societies often forbidden for a prescribed period before hunting. Whatever it means it is a male determinant in the paintings and the 'White Lady' has it in precisely the right place. The penis is not shown but since it must be the left leg which is forward the organ would be behind it. Close examination of the painting shows what may be the tip of the penis projecting beyond the vertical 'bar'. Herr Maack discoverer of the figure, had no doubt of its male sex and firmly states that 'there was no indication of female breasts'. His original sketch is shown in Plate xi. The accompanying figures are certainly a strange assortment, performing apparently some ritual, and there are many similar figures in other rock shelters in the Brandberg and elsewhere in South-West Africa. Who they are we can only guess.

In one sense no doubt 'foreigners' are represented. All the peoples of South-West Africa, except possibly the Bushmen, migrated from the north. Hottentots, Bantu and Negroid Berg Dama arrived in many waves in various stages of culture and much hybridisation took place. There is no reason to look further than these and the Bushmen for the peoples painted on the rocks. No object certainly identifiable in the paintings does not belong to sub-Saharan Africa and in the scores of once inhabited shelters which the Abbé and his helpers visited no single artefact was found not of Bantu, Bushman or Hottentot manufacture, except earlier stone implements.

Another group of paintings thought by the Abbé to show foreign visitors in ancient times is near St. Theresa Mission in Northern Basutoland[85]. Among many other paintings in a variety of styles and forming several layers, are a number of figures wearing long cloaks over their arms and down to their ankles (See Plate 26 and Fig. 12). The bottom edge of the cloaks is serrated and the outline is filled in with zigzag lines. The heads are highly conventionalised and the figures show at the shoulder the top of a large quiver well filled with arrows. It was because of the large quivers which he considered to be of Mesopotamian type and because of the long cloaks which are represented in a way somewhat similar to the sheepskin cloaks in Sumerian art, that the Abbé suggests that these figures are Sumerians. The paintings would thus have to be some 4,500 years old. It has already been mentioned that the Bantu wore long skin cloaks. These were often made of the skins of several small furred animals, such as jackals, wildcats or rock-rabbits, sewn together. The Bantu in Basutoland traded with Bushmen, the better hunters, for these skins, and it is quite possible (though not historically recorded) that the Bushmen in these bitter uplands wore such long karosses themselves in imitation of their Bantu neighbours, or perhaps even before the Bantu arrived. Is it not more reasonable to look to the skin cloaks for the garments in the paintings and the artists' difficulties in representing fur as the explanation of the zig-zag lines, than to seek five thousand miles away and nearly five thousand years back in time for a parallel? Also the figures are not shod, which would be strange in civilised foreigners.

As to the quivers they are no larger in proportion to the figures carrying them than many worn by obvious Bushmen in the paintings. A little figure near the one in Fig. 12 (Fig. 13) seems to me to clinch the matter. He is carrying, as the Abbé admits, the same kind of quiver, and he is also wearing hanging back from his shoulders the typical short Bushman kaross made from a single buck's skin and seen in scores of paintings on the Natal side of the Drakensberg.

Against the 'foreigner' theory there is overwhelming negative evidence. The various kinds of figures which Breuil believes to be pictures of foreigners are found in at least a score of shelters in the Drakensberg and, on his own showing, also in scores of shelters in South-West Africa. In none of these caves, or in any of those in the Kei River valley from which Schweiger drew his examples, was any artefact found which was 'foreign' in Breuil's sense though most of the shelters had every evidence of long occupation.

A further question of much interest is whether any marine animals are represented in rock paintings far inland. It has already been mentioned that the half-human, half-fish-like creatures near Oudtshoorn (Plate 11) are probably based on the dugong and an excellent painting of a sperm whale is painted on a grave stone found in one of the Zitzikama caves and now in the Port Elizabeth Museum; but both these sites are near the sea.

In 1944 the Abbé Breuil read a paper in which he identified a painting near Ladybrand in the Orange Free State as a whale and other paintings in the same district as dolphins[86] (see Fig. 15). L. H. Wells in the following year recorded other paintings in the Orange Free State (at Caledon Poort near Bethlehem) which he and the Abbé also considered to represent dolphins[87] (Fig. 15). Although Wells points out several discrepancies between the paintings and the actual form of the animals this was accepted as natural in a work done from memory long after seeing the subject.

As the Ladybrand dolphins were accepted as such also by Professor C. van Riet Lowe and Professor van der Horst, then the Head of the Department of Zoology at the University of the Witwatersrand, I accepted the theory myself in *Rock Paintings of the Drakensberg* but pondering the matter further after I had visited the sites I was assailed by doubts. The sites are very near water, the Caledon Poort shelter being only about 50 feet from a sizable stream. It seemed to me that before looking to the distant ocean for the creatures represented on the rocks the possibility of these being from the stream hard by should be explored. Undoubted fish are quite common in the paintings and the Bushmen as we have seen were fishermen. I therefore sent illustrations to Professor J. L. B. Smith (of Coelocanth fame) and outlined the problem. His reply was published in the *South African Journal of Science*, but as it is brief I quote it here[88].

> 'I consider it unlikely that these paintings were based on dolphins. Especially the paintings from Ladybrand district indicate a Mormyrid fish. The dolphin has no anal or pelvic fins as are shown, the small fins beneath the head on these paintings

probably indicate the pelvic fins of a fish. Further these paintings show a tail fin in the vertical plane of the body. In any case one cannot help wondering how any natives from inland could ever have seen a dolphin. It is quite uncommon for dolphins to be thrown ashore, but if a dolphin were stranded and it was seen by any inland native artist he would certainly have noticed and shown one of its most striking features, namely the strongly toothed beak: especially to primitive people that would have been one of the most remarkable features of the animal and the artists would not have shown the plain smooth snout, (typical of certain Mormyrids), seen in all these paintings. Against the Mormyrid theory is that the animal is shown with a short pointed dorsal fin on the back whereas in Mormyrids it is long. Quite often however the front part of such a fin stands erect while the hinder part is depressed and may be almost invisible. All in all therefore it is more likely that these paintings were based on some Mormyrid fish rather than on a marine mammal. At present Mormyrids are not known south of the Zambezi, but in earlier times they may well have occurred in what is now South Africa.'

Accepting Professor Smith's view we are left only with the Abbé's whale which he himself said to be a painting very faint and difficult to decipher.

The probabilities would seem to be against the marine animal theory but I am bound to add that there is a painting in the cave at St. Theresa Mission which looks very like a seal (see Plate 26). Its head is next to one of the Abbé's 'Sumerians' and is shown in an illustration to one of his papers. Several buck are painted over and across the figure but the earless head and flipper(?) are clear. Following the outline of the figure to the right one arrives a little doubtfully at Figure 14. The eye is clear and whiskers, not visible in the photograph, are also clear on the rock.

The question of the sea-beasts is still an open one and further possible examples should be sought. It is important because the degree of tenacity of the Bushman visual memory is relevant to the interpretation of other paintings. That it was not too bad we know from the galleon found by Townley Johnson in a shelter near Citrusdal about 50 miles from the sea[68].

Fig. 14.   Makhetas. A seal (?)

Fig. 15.   Fish or marine animals

A.   Rose Cottage, Ladybrand, O.F.S. Painting thought by the Abbé Breuil to depict a whale. After Breuil.

B.   Uysberg, Ladybrand. Paintings thought by the Abbé Breuil and others to show dolphins. After L. H. Wells.

C.   Caledon Poort, Fouriesberg, O.F.S. Paintings also thought by the Abbé Breuil and others to represent dolphins. After L. H. Wells.

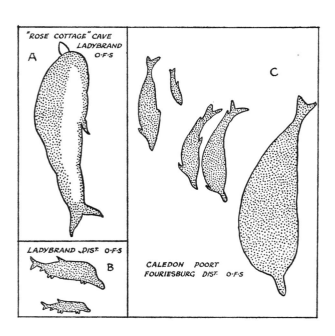

8
The Rock Art – its Age and Affinities

The dating of rock paintings found in open shelters is peculiarly difficult. In Europe the paintings often show animals which became extinct at dates approximately known and the cave entrances were sometimes covered by deposits roughly datable. *Art mobilier* which could be linked stylistically with the cave paintings was also found in datable deposits, even including some of the preliminary sketches for the parietal art. None of these fortunate occurrences aid the archaeologist in South Africa.

Many of the late paintings and a few petroglyphs can be dated by their subjects as these show Bantu, Europeans, cattle, horses, sheep, etc., the time of whose first entry into the area is roughly known.

So far in Southern Africa no rock paintings have been found below the ground surface, no animals have been certainly identified in the paintings or petroglyphs other than living species or animals which became extinct within the last two centuries, and no *art mobilier* has been found in painted shelters. There have been found buried in rock shelters without wall paintings some 'gravestones' with paintings on them[22, 76]. The provenance of all but one of these, i.e. from Matjes River, is uncertain. They all seem to have come from rock shelters in the Zitzikama district but they were excavated in the pre-scientific period of South African archaeology and the precise circumstances in which they were found were not recorded. The Matjes River example will be discussed later in this chapter. The only art on bone so far found in South Africa was on the shoulder blade of a lion in a cave at Knysna[22]. Conflicting accounts leave it uncertain whether the animal represented was a seal or an eland and it is not even clear whether the pictures were painted or engraved.*

A scapula provides a good flat, smooth, surface for a sketch, hence its use in China and elsewhere for divination, and it would not be surprising if others were found with art on them if more digging were done in the shelters. This may explain why Bushmen according to Dr Bleek's informants did not throw shoulder blades away after eating the meat but kept them carefully.

No rock paintings have been found in shelters which contained Middle Stone Age or Magosian deposits unless Later Stone Age material was also present, but they are found in hundreds of shelters which have *only* Later Stone Age deposits. For this and many other good

* Professor A. J. H. Goodwin in referring to this scapula stated[22] that it had been lent to the British Museum but was stolen on the return voyage. I was somewhat startled therefore, after writing the above, to find a small sketch of a scapula with figures on it in Col. L. van der Post's *Heart of the Hunter* and immediately wrote to him to ask its provenance. The sketch turned out to have been made from the original still in the British Museum and the Deputy Keeper of the Department of Ethnography, Mr. W. B. Fagg, informed me that it was bought from one Thomas Hedley in 1886 and was attributed to the Knysna caves. So it is undoubtedly the missing bone (See Plate xvi). It is 7⅜ inches in length and has paintings in black not easy to identify but including almost certainly a bird and a seal. Art on scapulae has been found at Altamira and elsewhere in Europe but this is the only South African example and it is good to have rediscovered it.

48

reasons there is no need to suppose any rock paintings to be of earlier than Later Stone Age date. The age-range of the petroglyphs will be discussed separately in a later chapter.

Radio carbon (C. 14) dating has been applied to deposits in two rock shelters having parietal art and to one in which a painted gravestone was found (Matjes River).

One case, that of the Phillipp Cave in South-West Africa[89], can be disregarded as there was nothing whatever to link the dated stratum in the deposit with the rock paintings, as several South African archaeologists have demonstrated[90, 91, 34]. The date of 3,368 ± 200 years B.P. is of interest only as indicating the age of the stone industry found in the same layer. This was a Later Stone Age industry resembling Smithfield B.

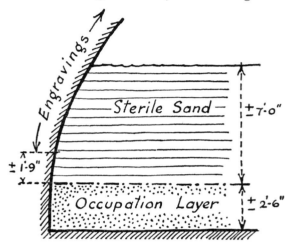

Fig. 16. Diagrammatic section through Chifubwa stream cave, Solwezi, Northern Rhodesia.

The second case is that of a rock shelter on the Chifubwa Stream, Solwezi, Northern Rhodesia. The rock art, which was first described by Professor Raymond Dart[92, 93, 94], consists of engravings of geometrical type such as long and short vertical lines, inverted U's or hairpins, loops, and cup depressions. Some of the engravings have had paint on them. Professor Dart who favours theories of foreign influence on the rock art of South Africa (see chapter 6) saw in these marks 'representations of human figures in a processional arrangement surmounted by symbolical and mystical signs which may originally have formed an inscription'. Some two thirds of the cave deposit was excavated in 1928 and 1929 but no description was published and the material recovered has been lost. The remainder of the shelter was excavated by Dr J. Desmond Clark whose report on the dig can be accepted with complete confidence. It was briefly discussed in my *Rock Paintings of the Drakensberg* but a further report by Dr Clark in 1958 makes a new appraisal necessary. The drawing (Fig. 16) is diagrammatic and made from Dr Clark's description.

The carbon, which was dated 6,310 ± 250 years B.P., was obtained from the lowest foot of the sand layer and the top part of the underlying layer and was in the form of small scattered charcoals. The occupation layer contained a stone industry of the earliest stage of the Natchikufan Culture, including two tools which might have been used for engraving, and some pigment. As there is no cultural material at all in the sand layer and the engravings are too numerous to have been done by any people in very brief occupation of the shelter there is high probability that the Natchikufan people executed the rock art.

Whether the carbon date can be related to the culture is, on the other hand, debatable. The charcoal was not found forming part of a hearth in the cave but in small scattered pieces and the sterile sand layer was, Dr Clark tells us, washed and perhaps partly blown into the cave from a shoulder of the hill outside. It is therefore quite likely that the charcoals were washed in with it and originated from an ancient and buried fire re-exposed by the erosion. The only alternative explanation for the presence of the charcoal in the sand layer seems to be that it was brought in by human agency but there are no other signs of human occupation in that layer.

From my specialised point of view as a student of rock art I find it difficult to believe that the geometrical motifs of this shelter could be expressions – and the sole expressions – of a purely hunting and food gathering culture. It would be unparallelled as far as I know in hunter art of any period anywhere in the world. Dr (now Professor) Clark has, however, pointed out in correspondence with me that the geometrical petroglyphs may not have been the only form of art of its makers but may have been accompanied by a plastic representational art in clay or wax which would not have survived. Also the C 14 date is much what he would expect for Natchikufan 1. The probabilities therefore would seem to be in favour of an age for these petroglyphs equal to, or not much less than, that of the dated carbon. I must confess that to me some doubts, perhaps irrational, remain. Two other sites with similar engravings exist in the Solwezi area. The excavation of even one of these could remove all doubts. Professor Clark dismisses Professor Dart's somewhat fanciful interpretations with the comment that it can be confidently stated that the engravings, which are all of a stylized, schematic nature, can in no way be considered to be an example of archaic writing nor do they represent long haired 'teddyboys' from Egypt.

The Matjes River rock shelter has already been mentioned. Situated near Plettenberg Bay in the Cape it is a big shelter 160 feet long with an occupation deposit in places more than 30 feet deep. The excavation of the shelter was begun in 1929 by its discoverer, the late Professor J. F. Dreyer, and continued intermittently under the direction of Dr A. C. Hoffman and Dr A. J. D. Meiring until 1953.

It soon became apparent that this was an extremely important archaelogical site. Thousands of implements of stone, shell, and bone came to light and scores of skeletons. Even more important, carbon which could be dated was found in the various layers and a painted gravestone was for the first time found in a controlled dig. This shelter had everything (except rock paintings on its wall) and the full report was eagerly awaited. It appeared in 1960 as a doctoral thesis written by Dr J. T. Louw[76] only to be received with disappointment and subjected to severe criticism by experts.

It is an archaeological commonplace that when a cave deposit has burials (and this one had scores if not hundreds), the acts of interment must upset the stratification. The dead could not be left on the surface and it is obvious that in fact they were not, but were buried with some ceremony. When a grave is dug, material from the bottom of the excavation is brought to the surface and not all of it returned with the grave filling; and some material from the surface will find its way into the grave filling. The age of the interment will not be that of the stratum in which the remains are found but will be the age of the surface from which the grave was dug. The age of the burial also cannot be earlier than the age of any object certainly forming part of the grave filling, but can be of any later period. Extraordinary care is necessary in such a case to excavate inch by inch, to determine exactly the level of the bottom and top of the

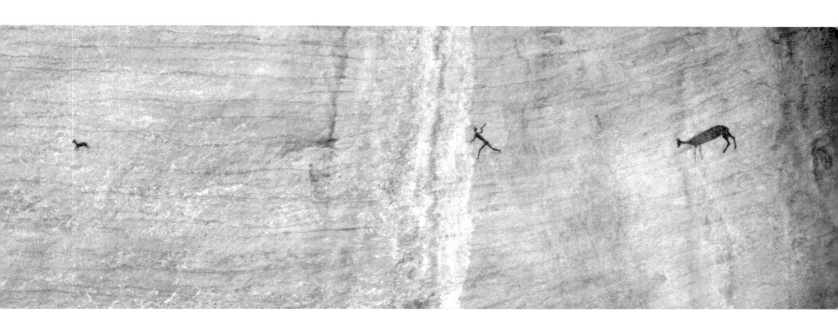

12. (top) Lorraine near Clanwilliam, Cape Province. Probably a man running down a young antelope, followed by the mother animal. The larger animal is 5 inches long.

13. (bottom) Abel's Cave, Cockscomb Mountain, Cape Province. A flight of birds (vultures)? and a crude elephant decorate the ceiling of this cave. At bottom left are numerous hand imprints. The hands are about 5 inches long.

14. The farm North Brabant, Waterberg, North-West Transvaal. Animal and human figures. The top animal is a kudu cow. The man at bottom left carries a bow. The kudu is about 7 inches long.

15. The farm Cradock, Waterberg. At centre a dance with one figure doing a somersault. At top a hand imprint, one of many in the shelter.

16. Rockydrift near Nelspruit, Eastern Transvaal. Part of a group of elephants, tsessebe and human figures. The elephant at centre is about 6 inches long.

17. Andover, Wodehouse district, Cape Province. Cattle and fat-tailed sheep. The bull or ox at top is in shaded polychrome and shows that this technique persisted into the nineteenth century. The bovine is about 8 inches long.

18. Ikanti Mountain, near Sani Pass, Drakensberg, Natal. Some of the marching figures in Plate xiii.

xvi. The only painting on bone ever found in South Africa. It is now in the British Museum. See page 48 for description.

xvii. Bosworth Farm, Klerksdorp. Petroglyph of lion, about 12 inches long.

xviii. Redan, Transvaal. Petroglyph design of circles and radiating lines. About 8 inches in diameter.

xix. Klipfontein, near Kimberley, Cape Province. Petroglyph design of circles and radiating lines. About 8 inches in diameter.

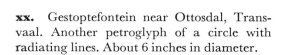

xx. Gestoptefontein near Ottosdal, Transvaal. Another petroglyph of a circle with radiating lines. About 6 inches in diameter.

grave and the nature of the grave filling so that many careful sections can be drawn. If this was done at Matjes River there is no indication of it in the report, indeed not even the position and depth of a single one of the skeletons is stated, and the two sections given show no detail within the layers, are difficult to relate to the sketch plan, and are drawn to a scale not stated but which appears to be about 1 cm : 5 ft, too small a scale to be of much use.

The layers of the deposit, denoted from the top downwards as A, B, C, D and E, all had skeletal remains in them but quite likely not, as we have seen, properly *of* them, and carbon was recovered and subsequently dated from layers C and D. The two dates from layer C are 7,750 ± 300 years and 5,400 ± 250 years and from layer D, 10,500 ± 400 years and 11,250 ± 400 years, all before present. Though the layers are thick, in the case of layer D reaching a maximum of 16 feet, the depths from which the carbon samples were obtained are not stated. Unless they were taken from the top and bottom of the respective layer and were shown by undisturbed stratification to belong there, the dates do not give us the limits of time during which the layers were deposited. Layer C could for example date from 2,000 years ago to anything over 7,450 as far as the information given in the report is concerned. This vagueness is unfortunate, as the painted gravestone – precious thing – is stated to belong to layer C and if it could be shown by undisturbed stratification to belong there and not have been interred into it with a body from a higher level, and further if its relation to one of the dated carbon samples were demonstrated, we could approximately date the stone and hence the possible beginning of rock painting in the extreme South of Africa.

It does seem highly probable that we can take the oldest carbon date of 11,250 ± 400 years B.P. as giving us the latest date for the beginning of the Later Stone Age, for all the material found in this shelter was of that period except for a number of Middle Stone Age artefacts which had been reworked into Later Stone Age forms and must therefore be given the later age for their appearance in this shelter. This gives a somewhat longer duration for the Later Stone Age than most archaeologists would have expected and only confirmation from another site can ensure its final acceptance.

Although the excavators of the shelter removed about 2,000 tons of material this represented only one eighth of the total volume of the deposit. It is to be hoped that some of the remainder will be excavated under rigidly controlled conditions by an *archaeologist* giving special attention to layer E from which only a few stone tools and flakes of uncertain classification were recovered. Skulls were found in this layer also but they are not described in the report and though ash was found in layer E this apparently was not submitted for C. 14 dating. Carbon dates from layer B would give us the upper age limit of layer C.

This rock shelter may yet yield the answer to many of our questions.

It will be apparent to the reader that any estimate of the time of the beginning of rock art in Southern Africa can, in the present state of archaeology, be little better than a guess, and the art of which any trace now remains upon the rocks may belong to a period much later than the beginning. An age of five centuries for the oldest *surviving* art is I should say certain, an age of twenty centuries quite possible, but longer than this unlikely for rock paintings or petroglyphs under the conditions in which they are found. These estimates agree fairly well with those arrived at by the four distinguished authors of *Prehistoric Rock Art of the Federation of Rhodesia and Nyasaland*[96]. They date the beginnings of rock art in Southern Rhodesia to the first millennium A.D. They suggest that about 1000–1500 A.D. their Matabeleland Style 2 art of monochrome silhouettes was passed south to the Union (now Republic) of South Africa, and about 1650 A.D., after the evolution of bichromes and polychromes, a movement of rock painters carried this art to the Brandberg. This incidently would give the polychrome 'White Lady' an age of no more than about three centuries instead of the three millennia claimed by the Abbé Breuil. As this leaves unaccounted for the earlier art of South-West Africa I will suggest an elaboration of this pattern of diffusion in a later chapter.

As to the latest art, the Bushmen were still painting in the Drakensberg until about 1880[34], until about the same time in South-West Africa[97] and until at least 1917 in Northern Bechuanaland[98].

The Kalahari into which the surviving Bushmen of the northern part of Cape Province were driven, to join others perhaps already there, had no rock and the art necessarily ceased. Paintings on skins may have taken its place for a while. Two Bechuanas told Frobenius in 1929 that Kalahari Bushmen, when they had killed an antelope, cut off a piece of the skin attached to the hoof and having scraped and dried it painted a small picture of the antelope on the skin, tied another bone to it, and buried the whole in moist ground near a water hole[20]. The purpose was not explained but it was presumably to beget magically another antelope to take the place of the one killed. No graphic art remains to the Kalahari Bushmen except scratchings on ostrich eggshells.

Bound up with the question of the age of the rock art of Southern Africa is the problem of its origin. It is hardly necessary to say that on this point there are two schools of thought. Both agree that some of the paintings of Eastern Spain closely resemble some of the art of South Africa (Fig. 17) and that there are some general points of similarity even between the Franco-Cantabrian rock art and that of Southern Africa. One school considers this resemblance satisfactorily explained as following from the fact that in both cases it was the work of peoples in the same state of culture, both working on rock with similar materials and presumably with similar purposes; and finds it unneccessary to suppose any cultural connection between Europe and South Africa. The other school, the diffusionist, believes that the rock painters of South Africa were indirectly the heirs to the palaeolithic artists of Europe. This is my own view. Looking at the whole picture of the prehistoric rock art of Africa one finds rock paintings associated with Wilton industries, or others similar to Wilton such as Smithfield C and Natchikufan, in most of South Africa, Southern and Northern Rhodesia, and Tanganyika; and in North Africa the rock art is associated with microlithic blade industries of broadly similar type. Some at least of the Saharan art also has similar lithic associations and, though much of this art is Neolithic, some of the earlier paintings – like many from Tanganyika – would cause no surprise if found in a Bushman cave in the Drakensberg. As already pointed out in Chapter 2 we have in any case to look to the north for the invention of the bow and arrow and probably other elements of Later Stone Age culture in Southern Africa. These and the art traditions may well have arrived together. This I repeat is not to argue similar age for the rock art at the two ends of Africa, the cultural diffusion or drift of peoples could have taken thousands of years.

The argument that similar conditions will independently produce similar art is found to break down if one takes a world view. There is little if anything in the rock art of the hunters of Patagonia or Australia[99] that could be mistaken for a pre-neolithic painting from Africa or Europe. All in all I think the diffusionists have it.

A   Morella la Vella, Castellon de la Plana, Spain.

B   Ebusingata, Drakensberg, Natal.

C   Gasulla Ravine, Castellon de La Plana, Spain.

D   Cradock Farm, Waterberg, Transvaal.

E   Gasulla Ravine, Castellon de la Plana, Spain.

F   Giant's Castle Game Reserve, Natal.

G   Tassili n'ajjer, Sahara, After Henri Lhote.

H   The Kranses, Kamberg area, Natal.

Fig. 17.   Some comparisons of Eastern Spanish and Saharan art with that of South Africa.

9
The Petroglyphs – Classification and Sequences

So far the terms 'engraving' and 'petroglyph' have been used indifferently as synonyms, which in popular usage they are; but it will be necessary henceforward to be more precise. An 'engraving' will mean a work executed by incised lines, a 'pecking' will describe work done by chipping the surface and 'petroglyph' will cover all methods of working.

All petroglyphs are intaglios achieving their effect by the removal of the dark patinated rock surface to reveal the lighter colour below. This was done by the means above mentioned and in some instances by *rubbing* the surface and even, it is believed, by *etching* it by painting on bird-droppings. The etching however was almost certainly not deliberate but incidental to the application of the bird droppings as a paint[100]. The peckings or incisions can be fine or coarse and very shallow or deeper; some idea of what these terms mean in measurement will be given later. Peckings and lines are very rarely found in the same figure.

Beginning with Mr M. C. Burkitt[11] all the chief workers in this field have striven to establish the sequence in time of the different styles and techniques. This has been a difficult task, for the palimpsests common in the paintings are rare among the petroglyphs and where they do occur the underlying and the superposed work are often of the same kind. Differences in degree of patination of petroglyphs *on the same site* provide a useful guide if used cautiously and the two lines of evidence taken together have enabled the sequence to be determined on some sites. It is by no means certain (to me it seems improbable) that there was a constant sequence applicable to the petroglyphs as a whole.

Miss Wilman's studies were confined to Griqualand West and a small part of Bechuanaland and to work on one kind of stone – amygdaloidal diabase – so her classification could not be expected to apply generally[14].

Mr Burkitt's sequence was based upon work done on several sites including Vosburg, Pniel and Halfway House near Kimberley, and Afvallingskop at Koffiefontein in the Orange Free State. He was accompanied on part of his tour by the late C. van Riet Lowe who later gave further study to some of the sites and included others not visited by Burkitt. This led him to suggest some revisions and extensions and to arrive at the following classification which was considered to hold good for all the sites and to incorporate Miss Wilman's findings:

TABLE 1

SERIES 1	A Simple and finely *engraved* geometric figures.
	B Finely *engraved* figures of animals in outline only.
	C *Engraved* silhouettes, the silhouette being filled in with incised lines running more or less parallel to the nearest outer edge.
SERIES 2	A Finely pecked figures (in profile and silhouette).
	B Coarsely pecked figures (in profile and silhouette).
SERIES 3	Finely pecked and rubbed figures.

SERIES 4   Modern. Metal graving tools, etc.

Series 1A, B, and C may be contemporaneous. There is nothing to suggest a chronological sequence. Series 2A and B have every indication of being contemporaneous, but figures in Series 1 only consistently underlie figures in Series 2. The partially pecked and partially engraved figure at Doornhoek is the only exception known. For the rest, the four series given are chronological.

Van Riet Lowe's paper read in June, 1936, was followed in the same year by A. J. H. Goodwin's *Vosburg: Its Petroglyphs*[100], still by far the most thorough study to have been made of one site, or rather group of sites on the same property. Goodwin's conclusions are summarised below but the descriptions of 'styles' have been very much shortened and the reader is referred to the monograph for details.

TABLE 2

PHASE 1   Early, deeply engraved.
Style 1.   Very deeply patinated cross-hatched designs. Objects too stylised to be recognised.
Style 2.   Animal forms in deeply scratched lines cut with a fairly coarse tool.
PHASE 2.   Heavily pecked.
Style 3.   Deeply pecked outlines, carefully executed. Animals and ostriches.
Style 3A.   As style 3 but filled in with attempts at body marking.
Style 3B.   Outline figures pecked all over with 'dashes' to follow the lines of the hair.
Style 3C.   Deterioration in form, the kind of animal being usually unrecognisable, but with more movement and humour.
         Note: This style may precede 3B.
PHASE 3.   Chemically made (by painting on bird droppings).
Style 4.   Whimsical animal and bird figures, mostly silhouettes completely filled in.
Style 4A.   Includes snakes, human and anthropomorphic mythical figures, and geometrical forms.
PHASE 4.   Middle engraved.
Style 5.   Deeply scratched, similar to Style 2 but less patinated.
PHASE 5.   Lightly pecked.
Style 6.   Similar to 3B with light 'dashes' but without the strongly pecked outline. Includes good studies of animals' heads.
Style 6A.   Weird, loosely-pecked figures, sometimes badly outlined with light scratches. Some better animal figures.
PHASE 6.   Mechanically rubbed.
Style 7.   Fairly good animal forms, the figures often outlined.
Style 8.   Very lightly rubbed; includes human figures, a buck and perhaps attempts at scenery.

The latest styles (9, 10, and 11) are scratched with metal tools by 'herd boys' and Europeans and do not concern us.

There is, alas, no close correspondence between Goodwin's and van Riet Lowe's findings. Both make the earliest work engraved not pecked but van Riet Lowe's 'fine' engravings do not seem to occur at Vosberg nor Goodwin's 'middle engraved' in van Riet Lowe's series. The 'chemically made', at Vosburg are not known elsewhere. The best combination of the two sequences would seem to be as given below. It has required some lumping together of types of work both archaeologists preferred to keep separate but avoids any downright contradictions.

TABLE 3

PHASE			A.J.H.G.	C.V.R.L.
1	Fine line and deeply engraved	a. Geometrical designs	*Style 1*	*Series* IA
		b. Animal forms	*Style 2*	*Series* IB, IC
2	Heavily and coarsely pecked	a. Animal and human figures in outline only or with body markings. The work carefully, sometimes beautifully executed.	*Style 3, 3A ,3B*	*Series* IIB

55

PHASE			A.J.H.G.	C.V.R.L.
2		b. As above, with deterioration in form but more movement.	Style 3C	—
3	Chemically made	Animals, birds, snakes, human and mythical figures mostly silhouettes	Style 4, 4A	—
4	Deeply engraved	Animal forms similar to phase 1b	Style 5	—
5	Lightly pecked	Similar to phase 2a	Style 6, 6A	Series IIA III
6	Mechanically rubbed; sometimes with engraved outline	Animal and human figures, rare attempts at scenery	Style 7, 8	Series 111
7	Work done by metal tools	—	Style 9, 10, 11	Series IV

In the early 1940's a group of sites having only true engravings became known in the districts of Rustenburg and Krugersdorp and were reported by van Riet Lowe in 1944[102]. They include finely engraved geometrical designs, animal figures and a few human figures, also, less commonly, coarsely engraved animals, the line amounting to a shallow groove, and one rubbed petroglyph with finely engraved outline. They are all patinated to the same extent and van Riet Lowe suspected no differences in age between the different types of petroglyphs. But to conform with his previous analysis he was inclined to rate the geometrical designs as earlier and the others as coeval with similar engravings elsewhere. They would thus conform with his Series 1A and 1B. This relative dating rests solely on the hypothesis that work of the same technique, even at widely separated sites and in different kinds of stone, belong to the same 'period'. The rock in this case is not dolerite or diabase but hornfels, an extremely fine grained rock with a thin patina, both characteristics which may have influenced the artists' choice of technique. This hypothesis can be accepted only provisionally pending more evidence. As van Riet Lowe himself explained: 'The study is still in its infancy and several sites need to be exhaustively examined and described before we can proceed with any real certainty'. This is still true. At least a score of sites need to be examined with the same thoroughness as Vosburg and the comparative patination, superpositions, and associated stone industries studied. This work should be done by the same person so that precisely the same methods may be applied in each case and the study should not be limited to the engraving site but in each case should include any living sites which may be found in the vicinity. Only then could we consider the relative ages of the different styles and techniques to be securely established.

A special kind of petroglyph not included in Goodwin's or van Riet Lowe's studies above summarised are certain geometrical forms of pecking widely distributed in Southern Africa. At some sites they include a large variety of forms, amongst which are always found designs based on circles with radiating lines or rays; sometimes the latter are the only designs at the site. Sites at which there are a great variety of motifs are at Munwa Stream in Northern Rhodesia[103], Mosamedes in Angola[104, 105], Redan near Vereeniging in the Transvaal[106], and Driekops Eiland[107], forty miles south west of Kimberley. The circle and ray motifs occur at the above sites and also at Bosworth farm, Klerksdorp, Klipfontein[14] on the Hartz River west of Kimberley, and Gestoptefontein, Ottosdal[10, 21, 101, 108], Transvaal (see Fig. 33 and Plates xviii to xx). The prevalence of the circle and ray motif out of so many conceivable geometrical forms seems to me to be a chance beyond the possibility of coincidence. Has it some symbolic significance, perhaps the sign of a solar cult?

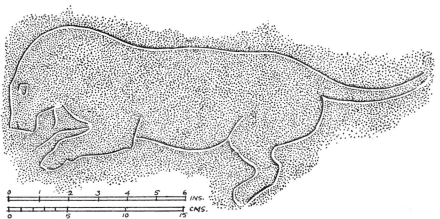

Fig. 18.   Africana Museum, Johannesburg. Engraving of lioness (?) from Doornkloof, Krugersdorp district, Transvaal.

Fig. 19.   Africana Museum. Engraving of rhino from same site.

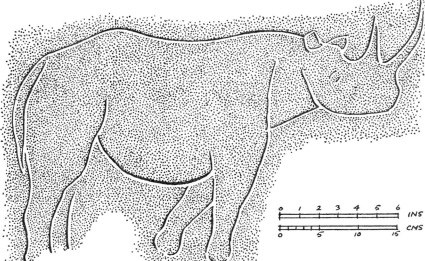

Fig. 20.   Africana Museum. Engraving of hartebeest from Doornhoek, Krugersdorp district.

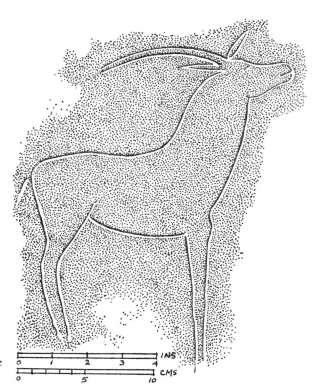

Fig. 21.   Engraving of sable entelope from Groot Moot, Krugersdorp district.

57

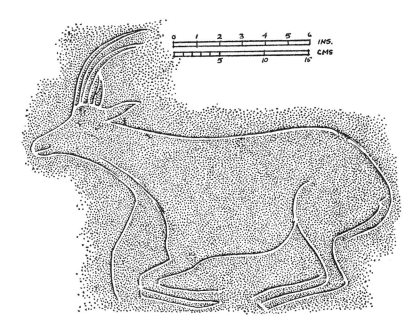

Fig. 22.   Engraving of sable antelope from Groot Moot.

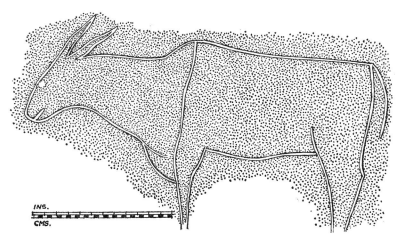

Fig. 24.   Engraving of eland from Groot Moot.

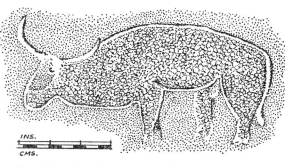

Fig. 27.   Old Transvaal Museum, Pretoria. Pecking thought by some to depict extinct buffalo. (See page 63).

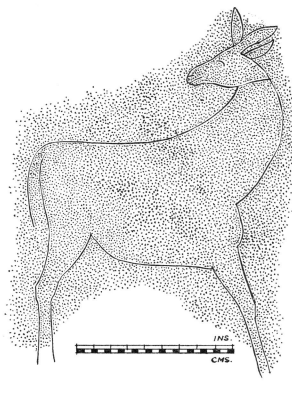

Fig. 23.   Engraving of indeterminate antelope from Groot Moot.

Figs. 25 and 26.   Engraved caricatures of elephant and hippo perhaps by the same prehistoric humorous artist from Groot Moot.

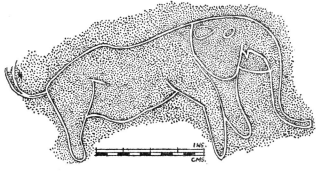

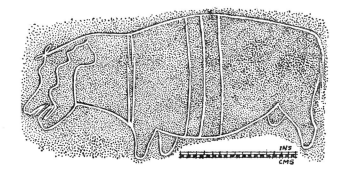

58

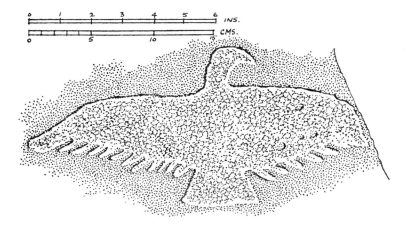

Figs. 28 (right) and 29 (above)
Old Transvaal Museum. Peckings of a giraffe and
a vulture from Sweitzer Reneke district, S.W.
Transvaal.

The Driekopseiland site had both Bushmen and Korana Hottentots living in the neigh-bourhood when Stow visited it, but Bantu have never lived there as far as is known. There is an older series of animal petroglyphs also present and an abundance of Smithfield B artefacts and debitage. It is possible that the Bushmen did the animal glyphs and the later Korana, moved to experiment by what they found there, but without artistic skill, made the geo-metrical peckings. They may also be responsible for the Klipfontein examples though these accompany normal naturalistic work. The Klerksdorp example looks much fresher (less patinated) than the typical petroglyphs with which it is found and it is possibly Bantu work, perhaps by a herd boy. Korana or other Hottentots, so far as is known, were never in the district. The Redan site also is outside Hottentot territory and it has been suggested that all the petroglyphs there are Bantu herd boy 'doodling'[106]. This is quite possible; the only attempts among them at animal glyphs are extremely crude and probably not Bushmen work. The Gestoptefontein petroglyphs, apart from recent European work, also include crude animal pictures and could be Bantu or late and degenerate Bushman art.

No single people could it seems have made all of the sunburst type of petroglyph in the Republic unless it were a Korana-Bantu mixture.*

The evidence regarding the absolute age of the oldest petroglyphs will be considered in the next chapter. This evidence is of three kinds: the associated stone implements and their distribution compared with that of the petroglyphs, the animals represented and the period during which they lived in the areas concerned, and arguments based upon the physical condition of the rock.

* A recent study I have made of the geometrical petroglyphs of South Africa, especially those of Driekops-eiland, and similar examples from other parts of the world, reveals a remarkable resemblance to the art of children of different races and culture before the representational stage is reached and makes it unnecessary, in my opinion, to suppose that there is any cultural connection between the sites at which rock art of this kind occurs, or that any meaning as pictographs or ideographs need be ascribed to these glyphs.

10

The Petroglyphs – Evidence of Age

The problem of determining the true associations of stone implement industries with petroglyphs is peculiarly difficult. Except for those found below the surface on the cave wall at Chifubwa Stream, no petroglyph has yet been found *buried* and to link art with artefacts when both appear together on the surface is not possible with certainty in individual cases.

The petroglyphs and the implements on one site could well have been the work of different hunter peoples who happened to use hill-tops and they may differ in age by centuries, even tens of centuries. In some cases they must do so, for even Earlier Stone Age material is sometimes found on petroglyph sites and such an age for the petroglyphs can by general consent be certainly ruled out. There is another reason, sufficient in itself, why stone implements of different 'Ages' should be found on engraving sites, for the dolerite, diabase, etc., which provided the engravers with their medium, were used also for the manufacture of the implements.

For the cases of known association our chief informant is Professor C. van Riet Lowe[16] who has pointed out that both Middle Stone Age and Later Stone Age material is found on petroglyph sites, but that the latter is much commoner. The Later Stone Age industries van Riet Lowe found associated with petroglyphs were Smithfield A and Smithfield B. These individual cases, as has already been pointed out, have little evidential value as they may be fortuitous and not enough work has yet been done for the associations to be reliably determined by statistical methods. But a survey of the distribution pattern as a whole permits some probably valid inferences. We find at once that there is no correspondence whatever between the distribution of the petroglyphs and of Middle Stone Age material[79]. The latter is almost ubiquitous in South Africa and though fairly common within the petroglyph zone is equally or more common elsewhere. For example there is an area of the Northern Transvaal and Natal about 100,000 square miles in extent which has Middle Stone Age material in abundance but which is without a single known petroglyph. Furthermore, although many Middle Stone Age sites, both open sites and caves, have been excavated, no indication has been found that the culture included any pictorial art. Whilst the possibility cannot on those grounds alone be certainly excluded there is nothing in the general pattern of distribution to support a belief in Middle Stone Age engravers. When on the other hand, we compare the known distribution of the A and B phases of the Smithfield (taken together) we find a fair degree of correspondence. The outline of zone 4 on the map (Fig. 3) which includes all the petroglyphs except a very few outliers, also includes a large percentage of the Smithfield B sites (about 70 per cent) and all the Smithfield A sites except three or four. Exact correspondence of distribution is not to be expected, as the presence of rock suitable to engrave on is obviously a limiting factor.

There is no other Later Stone Age industry found in the area except Wilton material, and its occurrences are far too few (about half a dozen sites) and too localised to be linked with the very much more widely distributed petroglyphs.

The picture as a whole therefore supports the evidence from individual sites that the petroglyphs were an element of the Smithfield A and B Cultures but the evidence of association with 'A' material is much weaker, for the number of 'A' sites in the petroglyph area is small and individual cases of its occurrence on the same site as petroglyphs are very few. Indirect evidence of this kind can perhaps never amount to proof but it seems to the writer overwhelmingly probable that all the petroglyphs except very late Iron Age (Bantu) work were the work of the hands that made the Smithfield B implements.

It has been advanced as an argument for the great age of the oldest petroglyphs that animals long extinct are recognisable upon the rocks, even that some creatures which went out before the end of the Middle Stone Age are depicted. If established this would of course be conclusive so the evidence must be examined in some detail.

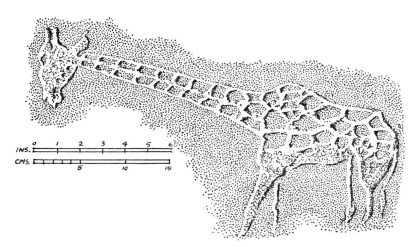

Fig. 31. Africana Museum. Pecking of giraffe from Sweitzer Reneke district.

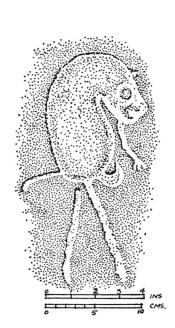

Fig. 30. Old Transvaal Museum. Mythical creature from Vryburg district, Northern Cape Province.

As already remarked the glyphic art is more variable in artistic merit than the work of the painters. In the rock shelters it is rare to find paintings much below the general level of work at the site: a petroglyph site on the other hand may have work ranging all the way from crude to masterly, even though apparently of the same period. The explanation is probably that since the shelters were living sites there was, as in all homes of taste, a certain minimum standard fixed for work which was allowed to appear on its walls. Few of the engraving sites however were lived on, being on or near the tops of hills in a climate for most of the year cold, and nearly always windy. The huts or 'skerms' would be about half way down the hill, as Africans build them still. Work of indifferent artists, beginners, and youngsters could therefore be tolerated: it did not have to be lived with. It is necessary to stress this variability because the species of animals represented is sometimes quite unrecognisable (as in Goodwin's Style 3C) and this bad drawing may easily result in a fluke resemblance to a prehistoric animal. A bad elephant may happen to be a good mastodon. Most animals of the Middle Stone Age differed

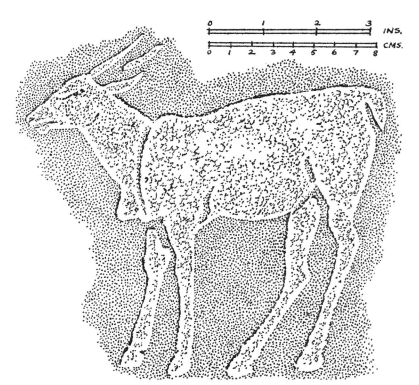

Fig. 32. Africana Museum. Eland in the most delicate fully pecked technique from Sweitzer Reneke district.

little from their Later Stone Age counterparts, except sometimes in size,and but a slight error in proportion of some feature could obscure the difference. Equally misleading may be the altering of a petroglyph by another prehistoric hand as happened at Vosburg[100] where trunks had been added to undoubted quaggas. In this case there could be no mistake; but the lengthening of horns for example could convert a modern buffalo into an extinct one.

One must not suppose either that all the animals depicted were adult and had fully developed horns, tusks, etc. or that the work was necessarily completed. It will be clear therefore that great caution is necessary in accepting prehistoric forms. The considerable weight of Miss Wilman's opinion was against the view that any extinct animals were shown[14] except some which remained until recently, such as the quagga which became extinct only in 1879. Professor Goodwin[100] shared this opinion. Professor van Riet Lowe while rejecting claims for mastodons, mammoths, and such like was inclined to accept one engraving as representing the extinct buffalo *Bubalus Antiquus*.

In 1928 and 1929 Mr Herbert Lang photographed and published in the *Illustrated London News*, with accompanying descriptions and general discussion many of the petroglyphs in the Old Museum, Pretoria. These were flatly stated to be 25,000 to 50,000 years old on the sole grounds of heavy patination and were stated to include mastodons. Also photographed but not published was an alleged extinct buffalo. As far as I know these claims received no support from archaeologists or palaeontologists but were generally criticised. Dr H. B. S. Cooke, geologist and leading authority on the fossil mammals of South Africa, emphatically rejects the identifications, and for reasons given later in this chapter even Mr Lang's lower figure of 25,000 years is an impossibly great age for any surviving petroglyph. Readers of the magazine were not told that before the photographs were taken the whole petroglyph within its outline was painted over with an oily substance applied with a brush, though this was obviously a possible cause of error. Such treatment was an archaeological crime, obscuring for ever the degree of patination of the peckings. Professor Goodwin expressed himself plainly but with restraint[100]:

'The likeness to accepted reconstructions of prehistoric animals may have been quite unconsciously increased by the process of adding oil or graphite to "bring out" the petroglyph, and to conceal chippings or scratches which were "not intended" by the original artist.

It seems important in a question of this nature, where an extinct species is concerned, to retain the surface of the rock in its natural condition without any sort of preparation for photography. A petroglyph ceases to have any scientific value once it has been tampered with, and the patina, technique, and form have been touched up.

The acceptance of a petroglyph as depicting an extinct species becomes less and less justifiable as the time-gap which has elapsed since the fossil lived increases. No zoologist would accept a new species described from evidence of a petroglyph alone: why should he accept such proof as post-dating the existence of an extinct form?'

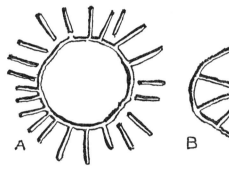

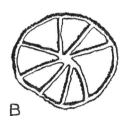

A and B   Driekopseiland near Kimberley, Cape Province. After C. van Riet Lowe.

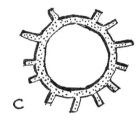

C and D Mosamedes, Angola. After Herman Baumann.

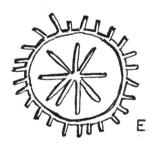

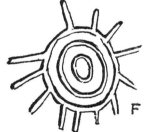

E   Driekopseiland, near Kimberley. After W. Battiss.
F   Mosamedes, Angola. After a photograph by M. A. de Pimental Teixeira.

Fig. 33.   Circle and ray motifs in the petroglyphs

Dr Erik Holm has revived this controversy in an article published in 1956[109], claiming the depiction of an extinct type of elephant, a bear, elk, horse and bison and the Middle Stone Age animal homoiocerus (a giant buffalo) in the petroglyphs. The photographs accompanying the article are not clear enough as reproduced to judge of the bear or elk, but the former, stated to be a *polar* bear seems extremely unlikely; nor is there the faintest reason to suppose that the elk once roamed the highveld. Bad drawing is quite enough to account for the oddness of the elephant and the horse could just as well be a zebra or quagga. The giant buffalo referred to is the one in the Old Museum, Pretoria, already mentioned. But 'the best example' claims Dr Holm 'is an engraving on the farm of Mr Penz about 12 miles south-west of Vryburg' which is said to be a bison. Dr Holm consulted Professor Goodwin regarding this identification and he quotes his somewhat sardonic reply 'the presence of a bison in a hot climate at the distal end of an even hotter continent, would be most surprising'. Dr Holm rejects Goodwin's counter-suggestion that the animal is a *sheep* on the grounds that it would then be the only example of a tamed animal in the rock art of the area that he knows of. Dr Holm then is unaware that on the same farm there is a clear and unquestionable representation in the same technique of a fat-tailed sheep, an animal first introduced into that region by Hottentots, probably by Korana in the eighteenth century. For a good photograph of this sheep I am indebted to Mr Walter Battiss. Miss Wilman referred to other petroglyphs of fat-tailed sheep from Barkly West. Dr Holm's drawing does not show us the rear end of the animal (it would be interesting to see what sort of tail, if any, is shown) but this would seem to dispose of Dr Holm's bison.

It must be stressed also that even if the elk, polar bear and bison were accepted as having existed in South Africa and as being represented on the rocks this would be no proof of the age of the petroglyphs unless the time of the extinction of these animals were also known. Only the pictures of the extinct horse and the giant buffalo would require us to accept an age of thousands of years for these pictures. The evidence for these is, in the writer's view, of the slightest.

With enough knowledge of the rate of patination of the rock and the rate of destruction of the surface, it would be possible to determine the age of any petroglyph within narrow limits: with the knowledge available this can be done only within age brackets all too wide, but still greatly preferable to unfettered speculation.

The rocks upon which, with very few exceptions, the carvers did their work, were dolerite, diabase, and hornfels in that order of frequency; all hard, fine grained, igneous rocks which patinate to a colour very different from that of the fresh unweathered stone.

The climate of zone 4 is what is to be expected of an inland plateau of its altitude (averaging well over 4,000 feet) and latitude. It is a region of hot summers and cold winters with a great diurnal range of temperature all the year round, the heating and cooling being often very rapid; of moderate rainfall (about 21 inches per annum) mostly in the form of thunder showers nearly all falling in the summer months, November to April, and of frequent dews and frosts. The engraved rocks therefore are subject to great and rapid heating, then often very rapid cooling as the cold rain or hail from thunderclouds falls upon rock often too hot to touch. During the six dry months, which include the windiest period, blown grit and dust picked up from ground only scantily covered with grass subjects the rocks to considerable abrasion. The petroglyphs, usually within a foot or two of the ground, get the worst of the dew and frost and being on hilltops, also get the worst of wind abrasion.

To illustrate the process of weathering by which the rock is eventually destroyed let us follow the fate of a piece of rock exposed on an engraving site. Let it be a rectangular block of dolerite freshly hewn from a depth below the penetration of the elements, and so retaining its original bluish-grey colour. Immediately chemical and physical processes begin their destructive work. Air permeates the surface to a depth of a few millimetres and water provided by precipitation and the frequent heavy dews penetrates to a somewhat lesser depth. Chemical

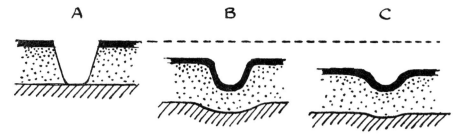

Fig. 34. Sections to show manner of weathering of engraved rock surfaces.

changes, principally oxidation in this case, take place and are intensified by the daily heating, the speed of reaction being in fact doubled for every 10 degrees Centigrade rise in temperature. As the rock is drying after showers and dews, dissolved material is carried to the surface and left there by evaporation of the water to form the true *patina*, less than a millimetre thick, dark brown (sometimes almost black) in colour, and composed mainly of oxides of iron and manganese. The leaching out of this material increases the porosity of the zone immediately under the patina, facilitating its decay, and this *weathered zone* changes colour to light brown and becomes considerably softer than the unaltered rock below. A section through an exposed surface of our piece of rock at this stage would show the state illustrated in Fig. 34 (A).

The rock is now almost black, perhaps with a reddish or purple tinge, and quite shiny, for the deposited salts have tended to fill in the minute irregularities of the surface and the wind has completed the polishing. Its shape is no longer rectangular for whereas the surfaces generally have been acted upon from only one direction, the edges of the block have been attacked from both the meeting faces and the corners from three directions. The corners therefore weather much quicker, and the edges somewhat quicker, than the faces and the rock grows progressively towards a spheroidal shape. The surface state illustrated in Fig. 34 will, barring accidents, remain constant because while the weathered zone deepens, abrasion will also be removing material from the surface. Fresh salts continuing to be brought to the surface will replace the loss from the top so both the patina and the weathered zone below it will remain fairly constant in thickness though continually retreating from the position of the original surface. The final fate of our rock will be destruction by the agencies already mentioned and by *exfoliation* of layers of stone caused by temperature changes, aided probably by residual stresses present in the rock, by the expansion of water which has penetrated the decaying rock and frozen there, and perhaps by the accident of fires or lightning.

These later events do not concern us for Fig. 34 represents the state of things when the prehistoric engraver set to work. It can be taken as certain that he did not cut deeper than the weathered zone for he had no tools with which he could have cut into the unaltered rock. This is so hard that even a diamond drill makes only very slow progress. He could in any case not have cut with his stone tool deeper than a few millimetres without cutting *wider* than he did. The depth could probably not have been greater than the width of the cut which is seldom more than three millimetres. But it is probable that he did go all the way through the soft zone to expose the unweathered rock and give good contrast between his cuts and the untouched surface. The tapering end of his stone tool must initially have made a V shaped cut subsequently widened out to expose a clear line of the blue-grey rock, as shown in Fig. 34 (B).

65

From the moment of completing the cut the process of patination of the incision will, of course, begin and it is because there is sometimes no apparent difference in the patination of the cuts and the uncut surface that great age has been claimed for the oldest petroglyphs. The argument contains its own weakness for obviously the patina on the cut cannot be as old as that which was cut through by the engraver – yet it is the same colour. After a time, therefore, during which the patina grows gradually darker, a stage must be reached when the colour remains constant and this time is the minimum age of the fully patinated petroglyph. The maximum age is the time taken for the surface to *degrade*, mainly through the abrasion of blown grit, the few millimetres necessary to efface the work completely. A late stage in the life of the cut will therefore be as shown in Fig. 34 (C). The edges will have weathered slightly and the cut grown shallower. To establish an absolute time scale for these changes is not yet possible with any precision but some reasonable estimates can be made.

The process of patination of dolerite and diabase is certainly slow. Inspection of walls built of cut stone forty years ago shows little change; but these are vertical surfaces. At Bosworth, Klerksdorp, early visitors to the site cut their names into the rock with the dates. The earliest is 1880 and though already patinated it is still much lighter in colour than the surface into which it is cut. About two centuries is probably a fair estimate of the time for dolerite and diabase to attain their final colour, though the thickness of the patina may still continue to increase.

The question of how long it takes for these rocks to degrade to the original depth of a petroglyph (say 5 millimetres as the outside limit) is one for the geologist. Approaching the problem as one who has been professionally concerned with the weathering of building stones and bearing in mind the extreme conditions of exposure in this case, the present writer is inclined to consider about 1,000 years the maximum possible time. Miss Maria Wilman and Dr Emil Holub both considered 600 years as the maximum age of any surviving petroglyph. Dr H. B. S. Cooke whom I consulted on this point said ' a few centuries, certainly not a few millenia'. He pointed out that the whole area in which this art is found is degrading fairly rapidly, the Vaal River valley eroding at a rate somewhere between 1 foot in 10,000 years and 1 foot in 1,000 years. Accepting the slower rate the top 5 millimetres of exposed rock would weather away in about 170 years and, making the most liberal allowance for the rock being especially resistant, it does not seem that this estimate could be multiplied by a factor of more than four.

It must be emphasized that the above evidence if accepted only proves that no *surviving* petroglyph can be older than say six or seven centuries. Others may have been done earlier and have been effaced, but this is an unnecessary hypothesis and therefore without scientific status. We have taken as our example an *engraving* on dolerite, but all that has been said applies equally to peckings and to work by both techniques on diabase and other similar rocks.

There is theoretically another way in which the age of the petroglyphs could be determined within wide limits. It has already been mentioned that implements are sometimes found on petroglyph sites made out of the same stone. Later Stone Age material is sometimes on the surface and on historical grounds may not be much more than a century old. Earlier material (Middle and Earlier Stone Ages) has not been found, as far as I know, in circumstances where it must have remained exposed for its whole life e.g. right on top of a hill. It is found only on the slopes, where it has been buried and is now being re-exposed by erosion. So its state of preservation is no help in estimating the rate of weathering of the exposed rocks on which the

xxi. Emil Holub at work quarrying petroglyphs for removal to Vienna. At top a fire has been lit under a petroglyph and water is now being thrown on the heated rock to crack it. Other assistants are at work with hammers, bars and wedges. Such methods are unthinkable today and removal by any method without a permit is illegal. From *Von der Kapstadt ins Land der Maschukulumbe* by Emil Holub.

xxii. Mpongweni, Underberg, Drakensberg. Shaded polychrome elands with human figures above and at bottom left a probable example of Bushman child art. The scale is in inches.

xxiii. Mpongweni. Caricature of Bushmen dancing and at top a woman, with her baby on her back, carrying a handbag. The figures average 4 inches high.

xxiv. Bellevue, Griqualand East. Elands and rhebokke. The largest eland is about 10 inches long.

19. Battle Cave, Giant's Castle Game Reserve, Drakensberg, Natal. Detail from the battle scene, Bushmen versus Bushmen. One figure with a large quiver crammed with arrows and holding a bow and arrows runs into the fray, while another lies bleeding from the arm and neck. The latter is about 5 inches long.

20. Good Hope, Underberg, Natal. Delicate painting of horse and rider dating from about 1850 shows that the late painting was by no means always degenerate. The scale is in inches.

21. Botha's Shelter, Cathedral Peak area, Drakensberg, Natal. A recumbent eland in shaded polychrome overlies the legs of tall human figures. Below and to left another eland in foreshortened rear view. The former animal is about 13 inches long.

22. Eland Cave, Cathkin Peak area, Drakensberg. Two running figures are a good example of Bushman skill in depicting movement. The figures are about 5 inches high.

23. Sandra's Shelter (shown in Plate 2) Kamberg area, Drakensberg. Black-backed jackal head up and howling. A miniature masterpiece. The animal is 3 inches long.

24. The same site as above. A fine shaded polychrome eland. The scale is in inches.

25. Tsisab Gorge, Brandberg, South-West Africa. The White Lady of the Brandberg. See also Plate xi and, for full discussion, page 43. The figure is about 15 inches high.

26. Makhetas, Northern Basutoland. At top left a cloaked figure thought by the Abbé Breuil to represent a Sumerian visitor to South Africa some 5,000 years ago. See page 43 for discussion and Figs. 12 and 13. Underlying some buck to the right is what looks like a seal. (See Fig. 14.)

petroglyphs are cut, or in judging the rate of repatination of the cut surfaces. If undoubted Middle Stone Age implements were found on top of a hill and the geologists could testify that there was no way by which they could have been buried for much of their existence, we would know that the stone and therefore also the surfaces of the engraved rocks of the same kind could remain little affected for about 11,000 years or more. I do not myself believe that continuously exposed stone implements could remain for anything like that time but they should be sought on petroglyph sites not spoilt by collectors picking up artefacts and dropping them again.

The Later Stone Age surface material found in association with petroglyphs, if systematically studied, could tell us much about the rate of patination and weathering of the stone, especially if cut across with a diamond saw to show the *depth* of the weathered zone. This could be compared with the depth of weathering beneath the cuts of petroglyphs by taking sections across fragments of some already broken, but the estimate of age thus made would depend upon the accuracy of dating of the Later Stone Age artefacts.

Seeking all possible evidence regarding the weathering of dolerite, I consulted Drs. Weinert and Clauss, geologists of the Council for Scientific and Industrial Research of the Republic of South Africa, who have been studying the properties of this and other stones used as road metal. Weathering experiments are in progress but it will be many years before they yield useful results. Dr. Weinert, however, mentioned one item of indirect evidence, arising from his research work in Europe. Dolerite and other lumps of rock found in glacial moraines certainly have all their weathered surfaces ground off by the action of the glacier which transports them. Although buried more than 100 feet deep below the present surface they were found to have since acquired a weathered cortex with a depth of about one millimetre for each thousand years since their deposition in the moraine. This was in conditions of protection from most of the agencies of weathering, and in fully exposed situations the rate must be many times quicker. Assuming a rate only twice as fast, i.e. one millimetre in 500 years, gives an age of not more than this time for two petroglyphs which have chips removed across the lines, for the weathered zone beneath the cuts is less than 1 millimetre thick. One of these petroglyphs was a dolerite pecking from Bosworth farm, Klerksdorp, for which I am indebted to Mr. J. L. Orford, the other a hornfels engraving now in the Old Transvaal Museum, Pretoria, from which the Director Mrs Roodt-Coetzee kindly had a small flake removed for study.

The sections were made by the Diamond Research Laboratory whose ready help is also most gratefully acknowledged.

What tools did the engravers use? Implements found at the sites and suitable as graving tools have been few and it is not certain whether they were in fact so used. Goodwin, referring to Vosburg, says 'In spite of constant search over a period of years I was unable to associate any tool with its type of engraving (petroglyph) with any degree of certainty'. E. J. Dunne stated that 'The Bushmen with silicious stones (quartz, chalcedony, agate, etc.) scratch the outline of animals, men, etc., on the smooth surface and rub away on the contour lines until quite a deep groove is produced' The present writer found a piece of highly crystalline quartz next to an engraving. Dr Emil Holub tells us[4] 'I succeeded in getting several of the curious tools consisting of triangular pieces of flint with which the outlines of the engravings are cut'. The pieces however could not have been flint: they were perhaps chert. There need be no mystery about the type, material or manner of use of the tool used for the engravings. Dunne's description is quite adequate except that the material need not have been other than the rock on which the engravings were done for a flake of the unweathered rock will always cut the weathered crust.

Miss Wilman however expresses doubts as to whether all the *peckings* could have been done with stone tools. Some of the coarsest peckings could have been executed with a stone pick but the fine work, and certainly the ultra-fine as illustrated in Plates 30 and 31 could only have been done by the hammer and chisel technique, placing the point (which must have been sharp) with extreme care. Experimenting with chert tools of the Smithfield cultures on diabase Miss Wilman found that they splintered without making any impression on the rock. It happens that the petroglyph area of Griqualand West, which Miss Wilman studied so thoroughly, corresponds fairly closely with diamond-bearing formations and it naturally occurred to her (as it had to F. von Luschan[111]) that these gems might have been used as tools. With the cooperation of a diamond cutter she found that a piece of boart held obliquely and struck with a hammer would do the job. The boart had however first to be mounted in a steel holder and it seems unlikely that the prehistoric artists could have made a satisfactory holder. Moreover the diamond is seldom found in nature with a sharp edge. Experts of the Diamond Research Laboratory consulted on this point told me that Miss Wilman's diamond cutter must have been very lucky. Unless struck at exactly the right angle related to its internal structure a diamond will shatter.

I have already mentioned Mr Borbereki's experiments performed at my request. He found it simple to make an exact replica of an engraving using only sharp flakes of the same stone and working the edge to and fro to make the groove. The coarse peckings also are easy to do with a piece of the same stone used as a pick, turning it in the hand so as always to bring a sharp point to bear. The fine peckings (see Plates 30 and 31) could only be done by using the implement as a chisel, very carefully placed, and renewing the point frequently.

II

Who Were the Engravers?

The study of the distribution of stone industries in relation to the prehistoric art, outlined in Chapter 10, makes it highly probable that the petroglyphs all belong to the Later Stone Age, and the supporting evidence of the rate of weathering of the rocks given in the last chapter seems (to the present writer at least) to convert that probability into a certainty.

Now the only Later Stone Age people we *know* to have occupied the region of the petroglyphs are the Bushmen. They were gradually dispossessed of it in the eighteenth and nineteenth centuries by Bantu (on their North and East boundaries only), by Korana and Griquas from the South-West Cape, and by Europeans who began to cross the Orange River from the beginning of the nineteenth century. Some Bushmen lingered in the north-western part until about 1870. There may conceivably have been other prehistoric peoples unknown to us who preceded them or shared their territory in earlier times but when European explorers and trekkers entered these areas the only Stone Age people they encountered were Bushmen. The pastoral Hottentot people, the Korana, who migrated from the Cape into this region in the eighteenth century still used some stone implements but also had metal tools and weapons so they cannot, either on the grounds of their way of living or that of their material culture, be considered a Stone Age people. They were not there early enough to do the older petroglyphs but theoretically could have executed some of the later ones. This is improbable however as the petroglyphs are typical *hunter* art and domestic animals such as the Hottentots kept are very rare as subjects. I know of no cattle and only two or three cases of the representation of fat-tailed sheep. And though the early settlers at the Cape were from the first in contact with Hottentots and studied their culture and traditions, they make no reference to these people ever having been engravers or rock painters. The Korana especially seem to have been totally lacking in artistic ability.

There is ample evidence on the other hand that Bushmen were the authors of most of the rock paintings and probably all of them except a few later and crude Bantu imitations. *Direct* evidence that Bushmen were also the engravers is lacking – no one ever saw them at work – but the indirect evidence would seem compelling. The stone industry most commonly found on individual petroglyph sites and which agrees best in its geographical distribution with that of the petroglyphs, is, we have already noted, Smithfield B. This was certainly a Bushman industry although perhaps not exclusively theirs.

The pioneer students of the Bushmen and their culture, still in contact with the survivors of the race in the Republic and able to question them, had no doubts that Bushmen were engravers as well as painters. D. R. Kannemeyer, G. W. Stow, E. J. Dunne, L. Peringuey, Dorothea Bleek and F. von Luschan all expressed this conviction and Dr W. H. I. Bleek was told by a Bushman in 1875 that his father had chipped pictures of gemsbok, quagga, etc., into

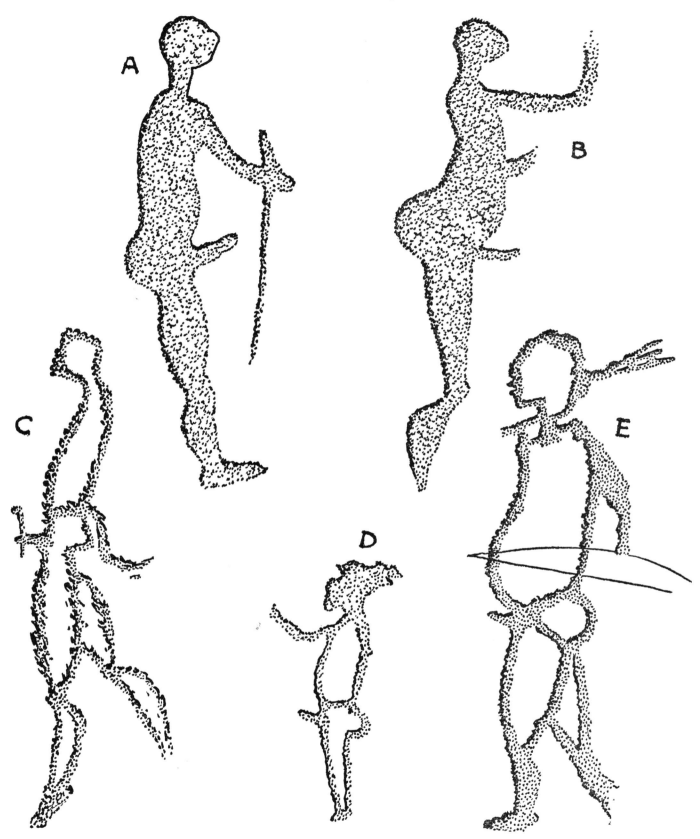

Fig. 35.   Human figures in petroglyphs

A. and B.   Kinderdam, Vryburg district. Northern Cape Province. After M. Wilman
C. and E.   Bosworth, near Klerksdorp, Transvaal
D.   Kuruman River, Northern Cape Province. After L. Peringuey

the rocks. Miss Wilman, after much careful consideration, also accepted this view. It is only recently that some writers have made a mystery of this question.

Study of the human figures among the petroglyphs yields further supporting evidence (Fig. 35). Most of them are too highly conventionalised and too little detailed to give any indication of race but many do show the hypertrophy of the buttocks (steatopygia) and the semi-erect male organ, characteristic only of the Bushmen and Hottentots, and some carry bows and arrows, the weapon of both these races. Excluding the Hottentots for the reasons already given leaves the Bushmen again indicated as the authors of the petroglyphs.

As already mentioned, other types of Later Stone Age man, such as those whose remains have been found in the Cape caves, may theoretically have roamed the region of the petroglyphs. There is however no evidence of this unless Boskop Man himself was of that period.

Though skeletal remains of modern Bushman type have been found at petroglyph sites it has not been possible definitely to link them with the petroglyphs. These uncertainties must be as maddening to the reader as they are to the writer. Why cannot my friends of the Archaeological Survey find buried on an engraving site the remains of an ancient artist grasping in one skeleton hand a stone engraved in the oldest technique, in the other hand the engraving tool with a layer of datable carbon above and below? In the meantime it is reasonable to infer that Bushman artists certainly made most and probably made all of the Stone Age petroglyphs. But more uncertainties lie ahead, problems which can be solved, if at all, only by the careful weighing of much evidence, some of it conflicting and all of it indirect. The next problem, then, is whether the Bushman engravers were of the same tribes as those who made the rock paintings or from a different branch of the Bushman race.

George William Stow, noting the almost complete geographical separation of the paintings and petroglyphs (see chapter 1) and that the former were found only in rock shelters and the latter on open hilltops, conceived the theory that there were two divisions of the Bushman race, the koppie-dwelling engravers and the cave-dwelling painters, and that these migrated separately from the north[31]. The sculptors, as Stow called them, were supposed to have passed to the east of Lake Victoria down through what are now Tanganyika, Northern and Southern Rhodesia, Bechuanaland, the Transvaal and Orange Free State to the Orange River. The painters were thought to have passed to the west of Lake Victoria through the territories now Angola and South-West Africa to the Western and Southern Cape, thence into our painting zone 2. This fitted well enough the facts then known but Stow extrapolated too far. We know that almost continuously along the route of Stow's *engravers* there are abundant rock paintings and comparatively few petroglyphs. And in South-West Africa, athwart the painter's path, lie paintings and petroglyphs in approximately equal quantity. The notion of two branches of the Bushman race divided as Stow suggested has therefore long since had to be abandoned, but cave-dwelling painter tribes and koppie-dwelling engraver tribes within the Republic of South Africa remained a theoretical possibility. Indeed it had much to recommend it, for it explained the separation of the arts and why the stone implements associated with the two arts also differ.

But the 'different tribe' theory has its serious weaknesses. In the first place it is difficult to believe that the tribes would, during the several centuries in which both practised their art, stick so strictly to the same territory. They were semi-nomadic hunters and some ebb and flow of boundaries is to be expected. And although it can be argued that the painters, accustomed to living in caves, would not leave the areas in which caves are found, there would seem to be no reason why the engravers should not enter the cave areas even if they chose not to live in the shelters.

Then there is the objection that the extreme specialisation which the theory requires – painters who never engraved *and* engravers who never painted – is unlikely. It has little support from the prehistory or history of art in other times and places. That there would be some individuals who preferred only to paint or only to engrave is reasonable, but that all the artists of a tribe should only paint or all only engrave seems against all probability. Also it is rather too much of a coincidence that the largest concentration of rock paintings in the world (zone 2) and the largest concentration of petroglyphs (zone 4) should be immediately contiguous without being the work of the same people. But coincidences do happen!

Some support of Stow's theory came later from D. F. Ellenberger and J. C. MacGregor in their book *History of the Basuto* in which they state that the Basuto recognised two branches of the Bushman race, the carvers and the painters. The joint authors uncritically accepted all Stow's ideas including those on totemism among the Bushmen and other ideas now known to be erroneous. It is to be feared that by their manner of questioning they may themselves have put the idea into Basuto heads when the latter only meant that Bushmen were painters and engravers. And as these authors identify the Bushmen with a lost tribe of Canaanites and support the King Solomon's mines theory of the origin of Zimbabwe, their critical powers are somewhat suspect.

The theory I incline to is this: the petroglyphs of zone 4 and the paintings of zone 2 were the work of the same tribe or tribes of Bushmen moving freely from zone to zone, possibly seasonally, and adapting their art and stone industries to the circumstances of different terrain. One objection can be raised to this theory. Why did the artists not paint in the engraving area or engrave in the painting area? To take these questions separately: why did the artists not paint on the open hilltops? Perhaps they did, in which case the question falls away. It is quite possible that some paintings were done and have disappeared and it is also possible that some petroglyphs were originally coloured in. There is some evidence of this. Miss Wilman in a letter to L. Peringuey informed him that the people who took her to some engravings at Warrenton (near Kimberley) stated that the petroglyphs used to be coloured. 'This', she commented, 'might account for the habit people have in these parts of speaking of the engravings as paintings.'[116] And van Riet Lowe wrote, concerning the Maanhaarand engravings:[102]

> 'In a certain light, the rock surface enclosed by the engraved line of some of the figures appears to differ from the natural rock surface that surrounds them. This has led some competent judges to suspect that some of the engravings may have been painted and that the colour differences within and without the outlines of the figures referred to are due to the chemical effect of the paint on the rock.'

But if no paintings were done on the koppie rocks it is not hard to suggest the reason: the artists reserved their painting for the rock shelters, wishing, like all artists, that their work should last.

The answer to the second question is less obvious. Why no engravings in the shelters? The rocks chosen to engrave upon – dolerite, diabase, hornfels, etc., have a thin dark brown or reddish patina on the bluish or grey rock (see chapter 10). Cutting through this gives a fine intaglio effect of blue or grey lines or peckings on a dark background. The cave sandstone of the shelters however does not patinate in this way and gives poor contrast between cut and uncut surfaces. This is the reason, I believe, why the artists preferred to paint in the rock shelters.* I think it is necessary also to conclude that they preferred to paint anyway and engraved only when conditions were not suitable for painting, for there are very numerous dolerite dykes in zone 2 on which they could have engraved if they had wished.

There is one other objection to the hypothesis that the petroglyphs were the work of the painters of zone 2. The stone industry most common in the petroglyph area as a whole, and found most often in association with that art in individual cases, is Smithfield B; whilst the industries associated with the paintings of zone 2 are Smithfield N on the Natal side of the Drakensberg and Smithfield C, with a very few occurrences of Wilton, to the west of the Berg in the region adjacent to the petroglyphs. This seems at first sight to support the belief that the painters and engravers belonged to different cultures, but the 'B' and 'C' variations of the Smithfield do not differ greatly. A typical assemblage of either includes many artefacts that could just as well be classified with the other; the 'B' artefacts which do not occur in 'C' assemblages are almost invariably made from the lydianite abundant in the petroglyph area but scarce in zone 2, where the material is usually chalcedony, quartz, jasper and chert. This difference of available material is quite sufficient in my view to account for the differences between Smithfield B and C.

Professor C. van Riet Lowe, the pioneer in the study of the Smithfield industries of the Orange Free State and their classification, himself considered the differences between the 'B' and 'C' phases to be mainly due to the influence of the local materials. In striking confirmation of this view he found that 'B' artefacts were larger where only lydianite was available and smaller (more like 'C') where chalcedony, chert, etc., were also to hand. It is not necessary therefore to attribute the typological differences between the 'B' and 'C' industries to their having been the work of different peoples or different tribes.

Occurrences of both rock paintings and petroglyphs on the same site being extremely rare it was of great interest to me, when visiting an engraving site in the Tarkestad District in the company of Miss Courtney-Latimer and Miss de Lange of the East London Museum, to find concealed behind bushes in a small rock shelter only about 100 yards away from the engravings a number of rock paintings. Even more interesting was the fact that profusely scattered around the engravings and also immediately under the paintings were stone implements of precisely the same kind – a rather amorphous late Smithfield – and there was no other kind of Later Stone Age material on the site. That the same people were at least sometimes both painters and engravers seems sufficiently proved.

There is one further source of evidence bearing on this problem; this is compara-

* The painted engravings since found by the writer in a Cave Sandstone rock shelter in the Limpopo valley may be thought to be the exception which proves the rule. Those engravings in the shelter which were never painted or from which the paint has disappeared are very difficult to spot and not visually interesting. It is suggested that the artist having made them as engravings was disappointed in the result and therefore coloured in some or all of them.

tive study of the two arts to note their differences and resemblances. This will be considered in the next chapter, but it should be borne in mind that even if the same artists executed both, the resemblance cannot be expected to be close: the utterly different methods of execution alone would preclude this. In addition there is the small size of the engraved rocks compared with the huge 'canvasses' of the rock shelters. We must therefore not expect to find scenes or groups in the petroglyphs as in the paintings; and we seldom do. Nor must we expect the same fauna to be represented: rhinos for example, which are animals of the plains, are common in the petroglyphs but rare in the rock paintings of the mountainous areas. The question is whether, having regard to the *inevitable* differences, the resemblances are sufficient for the petroglyphs and paintings to be the work of the same tribes. If my theory is correct the petroglyphs should resemble the paintings of zone 2 more than they do those of the other painting areas.

In view of the weight of the evidence that the engravers were Bushmen and of the same tribes (or at least culture) as the neighbouring painters it may be thought that I have been labouring the obvious, but this is apparently not so. Articles in magazines and even in scientific journals, and letters in the newspapers frequently appear announcing that the petroglyphs and/or the paintings (or most of them) were not the work of Bushmen but of Boskop Man, the Bantu, the Korana, unidentified 'Rock Men' and 'Cave Men', or mysterious foreigners. These theories are regularly demolished, but, Phoenix-like, rise after an interval renewed and vigorous.

27. Experimental re-creation of a petroglyph by sculptor Zoltan Berbereki to show how it looked when newly made and what tool might have been used. The original engraving is at Doornhoek Farm, Krugersdorp district, Transvaal. (See page 68).

28. Bosworth Farm, Klerksdorp, Transvaal. Petroglyph of hippo in pecked technique. About 12 inches long.

29. Same site. Delicate pecking of browsing buck. About 9 inches long.

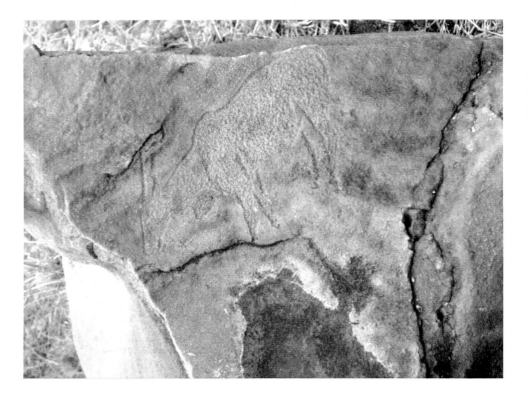

30. Sweitzer Reneke district, South-West Transvaal. Fine pecking of an eland. About 14 inches long.

31. Old Transvaal Museum, Pretoria. A superb example of the fully evolved delicate pecking. The eland is about 15 inches long. From Sweitzer Reneke district.

32. The Meads, Griqualand East, Cape Province. Elands in various aspects, including a remarkable foreshortened rear view. The latter about 5 inches high.

33. Bellevue, Griqualand East, Cape Province. Unshaded polychrome eland with
a tiny figure of a hunter above its rump. The eland is about 15 inches long.

12

The Two Arts – Some Comparisons

Comparison of the petroglyphs with the paintings as a whole reveals a general similarity. This is only to be expected: both were Stone Age hunter arts. The same conventionalisation of the human figure contrasting with naturalistic representation of animals occurs in both arts; the same absence of scenery, extreme rarity of perspective and preference for representation in profile, are observed.

There is one notable difference of subject between the petroglyphs and the paintings of all areas of the Republic of South Africa: that is the comparatively frequent depiction of plants and trees by the engravers and the great scarcity of *paintings* of such subjects. Perhaps the explanation is that the engraver on his hill top was surrounded within a few feet by plants. He could look at them as he worked and they would suggest themselves as subjects more naturally to him than they would to the painter in his cave.

To compare the scale is not helpful. Paintings are found smaller and larger than any petroglyph, ranging in size from one inch or less to (in very rare cases) more than eight feet, the size of the 'canvas' being often the limiting factor. The dimensions of the rock obviously also set a limit to the size of a petroglyph and the longest dimension seldom exceeded three feet without having a prohibitive curvature. The smaller size of some paintings compared with petroglyphs is sufficiently accounted for by the difference of medium; it is comparatively easy to paint fine lines using a few stiff hairs from a wildebeeste's mane as a brush, but nearly impossible to achieve the same degree of delicacy with a stone chisel. There is in both arts a tendency to keep the picture in some proportion to the subject, to make an elephant bigger than a jackal, an eland bigger than a rhebok; in other words some idea of scale was in the artists' minds. But exceptions are numerous. It does happen that the favourite animal in the paintings of zone 2 and the petroglyphs – the eland – is depicted in most instances about the same size.

Comparing the sequence of styles in the painting of animals in zone 2 with the sequence in table 3 (chapter 9) and allowing for the differences of medium, permits the following tentative correlation:

PETROGLYPHS	ROCK PAINTINGS OF ZONE 2
Animal forms in outline, engraved. (Phase 1b).	Monochromes in lateral silhouette (no detail within the outline).
Animal forms in outline only, pecked, (Phase 2a)	
Animal forms in outline, pecked, with body markings (Phase 2a and 2b).	Bichromes in lateral aspect. Unshaded polychromes, also in lateral aspect.
Animal forms in outline, lightly pecked with full detail within the outline (Phase 5)	Shaded polychromes with full detail.

Phase 4 of the petroglyphs represents a regression to an earlier style in a different technique.

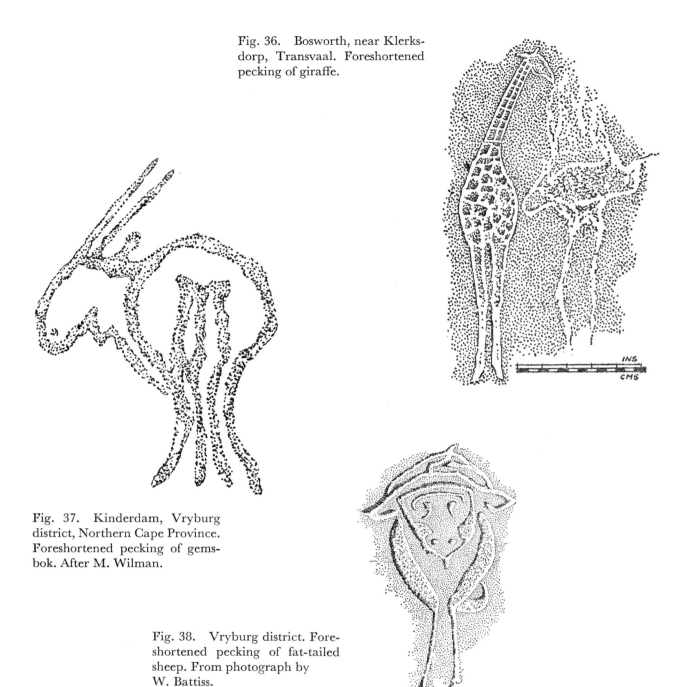

Fig. 36. Bosworth, near Klerksdorp, Transvaal. Foreshortened pecking of giraffe.

Fig. 37. Kinderdam, Vryburg district, Northern Cape Province. Foreshortened pecking of gemsbok. After M. Wilman.

Fig. 38. Vryburg district. Foreshortened pecking of fat-tailed sheep. From photograph by W. Battiss.

Such regressions occurred in the paintings also. The appearance of the outline engravings as the earliest is consistent with my suggestion that the first artists were painters who turned engravers, for they were accustomed to drawing in continuous line the outline of the animal. The coarse pecking technique and the delicate hammer-and-chisel technique would be natural developements as the artists explored the possibilities of this new medium. It is quite possible that these earliest outline engravings were coloured in, whereas it is, I think, out of the question that an artist would bring a petroglyph to the stage of detailed perfection shown in the late work (Plates 30 and 31) if he were going to paint it. He could put in the detail much more easily with the brush.

76

In the above correlation there is one apparent incongruity: foreshortening in the paintings only came in with the shaded polychromes, but in the petroglyphs first appears in the coarse peckings with body detail. This probably means that the first shaded polychromes with fore-shortening were coeval with the coarse peckings. It is a curious fact that foreshortening does not appear in the very latest shaded polychromes or the unshaded polychromes of the final phase. I know of no foreshortened examples of horses and cattle. Nor do I know of any examples of foreshortening among the lightly pecked fully detailed petroglyphs so it would seem likely that the late phases (without foreshortening) of both arts were contemporary. However that may be, the occurrence of foreshortening in the zone 2 paintings and in the petroglyphs (Figs. 36, 37 and 38) is one of the strongest reasons for linking the two arts for, with only one or two doubtful exceptions, which may be mere distortion, foreshortening does not occur in zones 1 or 3.

Another strong reason for presuming at least mutual influence between the arts of zones 2 and 4 is that both attain in their later stages a degree of complexity and of manual skill in execution seldom found, if at all, in the other art zones of the Republic.

The engravers more often than not preferred to depict animals standing still, sometimes grazing or browsing, but when they did show action it was done with a skill equalled by the painters only in zone 2 – another reason for linking the arts of the two zones.

It is instructive to compare the different ways of representing an eland in the paintings and petroglyphs. Rather uncommon among the monochromes, they occur frequently as bichromes, unshaded polychromes, and shaded polychromes. They are common also in all the petroglyph techniques. It will be noticed that in all cases except the monochromes a heavy line from the front of the withers marks the shoulders and base of the neck and joins the lower contour of the body below the dewlap. This line served in the bichromes and polychromes to divide two colours, the neck and head being almost always in a lighter colour than the body. Although it served no such purpose in the petroglyphs, except perhaps in some early ones if they were ever painted, this line is seldom omitted even in the crudest examples. Unless a coincidence, which seems unlikely, this is a convention shared by the painters and carvers and it provides still another reason for believing that they were the same people.

Although opinion on this point is necessarily based in part on subjective judgement and I should like to refer the question to a jury of art critics and artists (painters and sculptors) thoroughly familiar with both arts, my own opinion is that, making due allowances for the differences of medium, the two arts are not so different as to preclude their being expressions of one culture. Moreover I think it demonstrated that the petroglyphs resemble the paintings of zone 2 more than the other paintings, which on geographical grounds is just what my theory requires.

13

A Suggested Pattern of Diffusion

In Chapter 8 were briefly stated the conclusions of Rhodesian archaeologists on the diffusion of the Matabeleland art southward, first across the Limpopo and much later westward across Northern Bechuanaland to South-West Africa. It is generally agreed that the paintings of the Northern Transvaal can be regarded on stylistic grounds as an extension of the Rhodesian art zone into the Republic (see Chapters 1 and 6) and van Riet Lowe long ago pointed out the resemblances between some of the Brandberg paintings and others in the Fort Victoria districts of Southern Rhodesia[112].

Beginning from these acceptable conclusions it is worthwhile attempting to work out a pattern of diffusion of the styles of rock art which is consistent with all the known facts. These can be summarised thus:

1   All the rock paintings of Southern Africa are associated with microlithic blade industries of the Wilton-Smithfield C type.

2   Except for the late polychromes of the Brandberg, there is strong resemblance between the South-West African rock paintings and those of the Western and Southern Cape (zone 3), as the art only gradually changes its character from north to south.

3   There is greater resemblance between the paintings of zones 1 and 3 than between either of those zones and the intervening zone 2. This is chiefly because painting continued later in zone 2 and it therefore contains more of the later styles. The invention (or introduction) of the techniques of shading and foreshortening took place after the Bushmen were confined within this area, except for a few remnants outside cut off from the main body and therefore unable to share in the latest artistic developments. Simple monochromes and bichromes and unshaded polychromes of the kinds found in zones 1 and 3 occur also in zone 2 but are not common.

4   There are rock paintings in South-West Africa in appearance much older than the Brandberg polychromes and it would be difficult to believe that rock painting began there only in the seventeenth century A.D.

5   The distribution of painted hand imprints (see Fig. 39) shows them in Southern Rhodesia, North Bechuanaland, South-West Africa, and zones 1 and 3, but not in zone 2.

In working out the pattern it is necessary to keep one eye on the distribution of the microlithic industries and the other on natural obstacles. Only the central and Western Kalahari was any real obstacle to people in the rock painters' stage of culture: with so much better-watered territory to roam at will it is most unlikely that they would have entered it until forced to do so by surrounding enemies. First then I suggest two movements (from Matabeleland) of painters in the simple monochrome stage, one (probably the earlier) into South-West Africa, and the other into the Transvaal. These were the people of the hand imprints, small people,

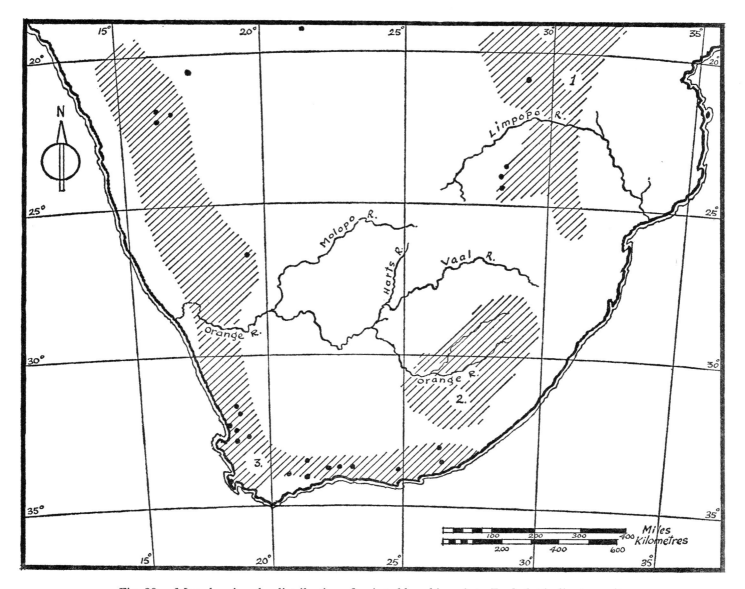

Fig. 39.   Map showing the distribution of painted hand imprints. Each dot indicates a site.

and cave dwellers by preference (Bushmen), (see on the map Fig. 40 the lines marked 1 and 2). Movement 1, which of course could have taken centuries, probably brought the first art to zone 2. I rule out the alternative that the art of zone 2 and the eastern part of zone 3 was brought by a continuation of Movement 2. It is unlikely that the Movement 2 artists would have stopped the practice of hand imprinting en route through zone 2 and then started it again when they reached the Eastern Cape. It is possible however that Movement 2 as well as, or instead of, Movement 1, continued into zone 2.

The petroglyphs of zone 4 are quite unlike those of Rhodesia or South-West Africa and, for reasons fully explained in Chapter 11, I consider them most likely to have been the work of the Bushmen of zone 2. Hence my suggestion of Movement 3.

Movement 4, in agreement with the suggestion of the Rhodesian investigators, brought the

79

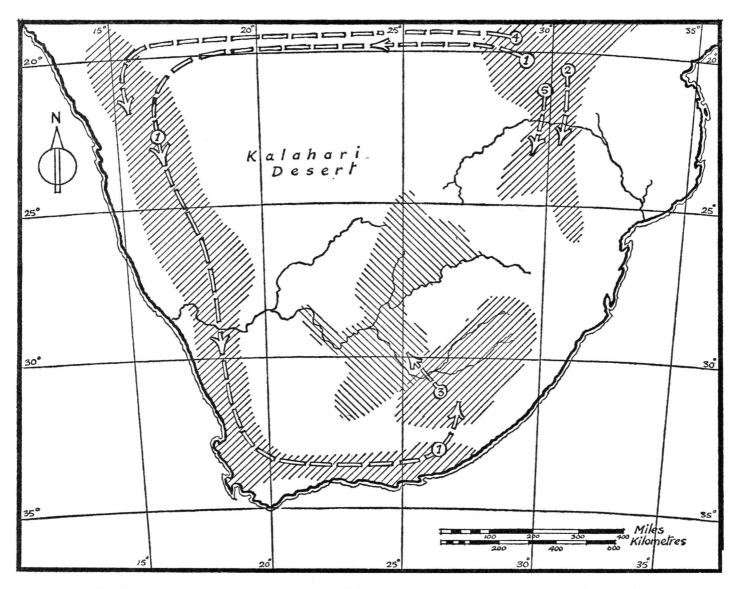

Fig. 40.   Map showing suggested lines of diffusion of the styles of rock art. (See Chapter 13).

newly evolved polychrome art to South West Africa. The few and cruder polychromes of zone 3 were probably independently evolved. Movement 4 was possibly of non-Bushmen or of hybrid people with a Bush component.

Movement 5, probably roughly contemporaneous with 4, accounts for the few unshaded polychromes of the Northern Transvaal. It does not seem to have gone south of the Waterberg, probably because rock shelters become very scarce there. This also may have been made by non-Bush or hybrid people.

Mr C. K. Cooke has recently discovered some shaded polychrome paintings in the Matopo Hills, and a single occurrence of such paintings in the Makabene Mountains of the Northern Transvaal about 60 miles south of the Limpopo has been known for some years[67]. These two sites may have some connection with each other (by Movement 5) but I doubt if these examples

80

have any connection with the shaded polychromes of zone 2, as there is a gap of 300 miles with at least a score of painting sites between the Makabene and zone 3 without a single known shaded polychrome and only one or two unshaded polychrome paintings.

The picture outlined above is admittedly largely hypothetical but it is submitted that it best covers the known facts. Even relative dating is still uncertain and definite dates for the earliest art in the various parts of Southern Africa, while probably not requiring the channels of diffusion shown in Fig. 40 to be altered, might require some of the directional arrows to be reversed.

A large question mark hangs over the Matjes River shelter. Further digging, carefully controlled, in that cave and others in the Southern Cape might well yield some surprises.

14

The Paintings and Petroglyphs as Art

'We can learn more of the essential nature of art from its earliest manifestations in primitive man (and in children) than from its intellectual elaboration in great periods of culture.'

Sir Herbert Read

It has been the intention in this book, by the inclusion of many illustrations, especially those from direct colour photographs, to let the art, as such, speak for itself. Comment will therefore be kept to a minimum.

The art, it will be obvious, is almost entirely perceptual, based on keen observation, not distorted by concept like children's art and the primitive art of civilised people. It contrasts with the latter also in never becoming repetitive and stereotyped as Egyptian and Mesopotamian art did. Even when the Bushman artist pulled off a masterpiece such as the jackal in Plate 23 he did not repeat it in the same or in another shelter. Creation, not mere decoration, was the aim in every work of art. Naturally the art, even of the same region and period varied in quality, including the work of beginners and of masters, but it seems that work below certain standard was not permitted to appear on the cave wall. This rule was broken sometimes to indulge children whose work is occasionally to be found low down on the cave wall and imitating, as well as the child could, an adult's painting above it (Plate xxii). It is interesting to observe that, although crude, the copies are not reduced to schematic form as those of civilised children normally would be. The significance of this was discussed in *Rock Paintings of the Drakensberg*. The comments which follow apply to the better examples of each period.

Artists and expert draftsmen who have accompanied me to many painted shelters have expressed amazement at the manual skill of the rock artists in achieving such beauty of line and delicacy of shading on the roughish rock surfaces.

Action was at all periods skilfully portrayed, especially in the human figures, with some deliberate exaggeration by way of emphasis; in the animal figures action is commoner and more spirited in the later work.

A painting or group of paintings executed at the same time was conceived as a whole, detail being subordinated to unity and the individual figures to the composition. Unparalleled in any other rock art in the world and indeed not equalled in any art until the fifteenth century in Europe was the Bushmen's mastery of foreshortening in zone 2 in the last few centuries of their existence there (see for example Plate 32). There seems to have been a quickening tempo in the rate of technical progress during that period: experiments in representation in depth with correct perspective were being made (Fig. 41), and who knows what might have been achieved had the artists remained undisturbed for another century?

Though technical skill and elaboration increased with the passage of time, it is doubtful

34. Mpongweni, Underberg, Natal. Three 'pin-ups' of Bush girls. Note the steatopygia. The figures are about 5 inches high.

35. Same site as above. A dance in progress, with women spectators on both sides clapping the rhythm. At bottom a horse. The human figures average 4 inches high.

36. Mpongweni. Part of scene in which Bushmen are driving off stolen cattle and horses. The cattle average 6 inches long.

37. Same site as above. Fine paintings of horses. About 5 inches long.

Fig. 41   Experiments in perspective:

A   Genaadeberg, Zastron, O.F.S. After G. W. Stow.   B   Kwartelfontein, Smithfield, O.F.S.
C   Tabamyama, Giant's Castle Game Reserve.   D   Drakensberg, Natal. After a copy by Mark Hut-
Four figures dance around another wearing a mask.   chinson in the Library of Parliament, Cape Town.

whether this increase in complexity in the art was accompanied by a rising level of aesthetic sensibility. This must be a matter of opinion, but some of the simple silhouettes have a delightful crispness and achieve as great an artistic effect with greater economy of means. This is not the place (and I am not the man) to attempt to distil from great art in its various forms the essence, if such there be, common to them all, but I would postulate that a principle of economy – the achievement of the desired result with the minimum of means – is found in some at least of the greatest graphic and glyptic art, music and writing. 'Painting' it has been said 'is the art of not painting, and writing of not writing'. Consider then the achievement of the Bushman in communicating to those of another time, race and culture his delight in the animal world and in the excitement of the hunt or dance. This is conveyed surely, with the

Fig. 42. Cartoon by 'Wimsey' from the 'Daily Sketch' shows that the idea of sympathetic magic is not dead.

utmost economy of means, leaving out background scenery, bodily detail and all else irrelevant to his theme.

As to his motives, whatever part magical intent may have played in the early development of the Eur-African rock art there is little to suggest it in the South African paintings. Some work may have had historical intention or have been done to illustrate a tale but in general the art gives strongly the impression of being *art pour l'art* executed for the pleasure of the artist in the work and the reciprocal pleasure of the beholder. It achieves this effect even on the alien observer of today.

The place of the South African rock art in the prehistoric hunter art of the world ranks only below the finest of the palaeolithic art of Europe and indeed the best Bushman work has in some respects a good claim to superiority.

Appendix

The following is a selection of the Notes and References used to prepare the map (Fig. 6) on page 24.

Number on Map	Date		References
1	1655	Jan Wintervogels expedition encounters Bushmen	*Journal of Jan van Riebeeck*, Vol. I p. 305
2	1660	Jan Danckheart's expedition en route northwards encounters Bushmen near Olifants Rivier	Ibid, Vol. III, p. 299
3, 4	1661	Pieter Cruythoff's expedition encounters Bushmen near Klein Berg Rivier and at 'Castle Meerhof'	Ibid., Vol. III, pp. 346, 347
5	1676	Burgers reported killed by Bushmen at upper Breede Rivier	Theal, *History of South Africa*, Vol. I, p. 226
6	1682	Olof Bergh encounters Bushmen near Berg Rivier	Mossop, *Journals of Bergh and Schrijver*, p. 85
7, 8	1685	Simon van der Stel's Expedition encounters Bushmen near Picketberg and at Great Doorn Bosch Rivier	Theal, *History of South Africa*, Vol. I, pp. 277 and 280
9, 10	1689	Survivors of the wrecked Stavernisse meet Bushmen about position of Keimouth and are told Bushmen are also west of the Amaxosa, i.e. west of position of East London	Theal, Ibid, Vol. I, p. 298
11	1689	Ensign Isaac Schrijver's expedition encounters Bushmen near position of Willowmore	Mossop, *Journals of Bergh and Schrijver*, p. 225
12	1694	Some Bushmen still in Drakenstein Mountains	Theal, Ibid, Vol. I, p. 352
13	1701	Bushmen steal cattle from Riebeecks Kasteel	Theal, Ibid, Vol. I, p. 385
14	1719	Raid on farm on River Zonderend	Theal, Ibid, Vol. I, p. 434
15	1747	Conflict between farmers and Bushmen on distant border of Swellendam district	Theal, Ibid, Vol. II, p. 64
16	1758	Bushmen raid into Roggeveld	Theal, Ibid, Vol. II, p. 100
17	1763	Bushmen raid into Bokkeveld	Theal, Ibid, Vol. II, p. 101
18	1764	Bushmen raid on cattle station on Zak Rivier	Theal, Ibid, Vol, II, p. 101
19	1770	Bushman raids widespread in this district	Theal, Ibid, Vol, II p. 102
20	1752	Ensign Beautler's expedition meets with no Bushmen until reaching the region of Tyumie to Fish Rivers	Theal, Ibid, Vol, II p. 133
21	1790	Jacob van Reenen's expedition in search of survivors of the wrecked Grosvenor finds the country between the Kei and the 'Samoe' (Tsamo) river inhabited only by Bushmen	Kirby, *Jacob van Reenen and the Grosvenor Expedition of 1790-1791*, p. 97 et seq.
22	1797	James Barrow finds signs of recent occupation of cave by Bushmen	Barrow, *Travels in the Interior of Southern Africa in the years 1797 and 1798*, p. 239
23	1797	James Barrow finds many deserted Bushman kraals	Barrow, Ibid, p. 268
24	1797	Conflict with Bushmen	Barrow, Ibid, p. 272
25	1804	H. Lichtenstein reports that Bushmen raiders from Roggeveld have been very active in this region	Lichtenstein, *Travels in Southern Africa*, Vol. II, p. 212
26	1804	Bushman stronghold still remaining in Bonteberg	Lichtenstein, Ibid, Vol. II, pp. 223, 224

Number on Map	Date		References
27	1804	Bushman raid on Hottentots at mission on Zak River	Lichtenstein, Ibid, Vol. II, p.226
28, 29, 30	1811	W. J. Burchell encounters 'wild Bushmen'	Burchell, *Travels in the Interior of Southern Africa*, Vol. I, pp. 205, 209, 272
31, 32	1812	W. J. Burchell has further encounters with Bushmen, He did not meet Bushmen further south than Kraaikop's Kraal (29) on this route	Burchell, Ibid, Vol. II pp. 26 et seq. and 61
33	1824	'Wild' Bushmen reported north of Hantamberg	Thompson, *Travels in South Africa*, p. 237
34	1830	Following thefts of cattle, commandos exterminate Bushmen in this area	Stow, *Native Races of South Africa*, p. 219 et seq.
35	1834	Area between Orange and Riet Rivers cleared of Bushmen by Griquas	Theal, Ibid, Vol. III p. 413
36	1837	W. C. Harris has six oxen stolen by Bushmen	Harris, *Expedition into Southern Africa* p. 313
37, 38, 39, 40	1839	James Backhouse encounters Bushmen still living at these places	Backhouse *A Narrative of a Visit to the Mauritius and South Africa*, pp. 341, 423, 444, 477 and 500
41, 42	1854, 1855	Fights with Bushmen at Thaba Patchoa and Vaalbank Spruit	Chapter 3, See text p. 22

For the final stages of the history of the Bushmen in the Drakenberg see *Rock Paintings of the Drakensberg*

Bibliography

The works listed below are in addition to those named in the text, which will be found in the index.

1 BOTELHO, J. J. TEIXEIRA: *Historia Militar e Politica dos Portugueses em Moçambique do Descoberta a 1883*. Lisbon 1934.

2 THEAL, G. McCALL: *History of South Africa*. London 1897.

3 HALLEMA, A.: *The Cape in 1776–7*. London 1951.

4 HOLUB, E.: *Sieben Jahre in Süd-Afrika*. London 1881.

5 PERINGUEY, L.: 'On Rock Engravings of Animals and the Human Figure', *Transactions of the South African Philosophical Society*, Vol. XVI. (1906).

6 TONGUE, M. HELEN: *Bushman Paintings*. Oxford 1909.

7 MOSZEIK, O.: *Die Malereien der Buschmanner in Süd-Afrika*. Berlin 1910.

8 JOHNSON, J. P.: *Geological and Archaeological Notes on Orangia*. London 1910.

9 CHRISTOL, F.: *L'art dans l'Afrique Australe*. Paris 1911.

10 ZELIZKO, J. V.: *Felsgravierunzen der Südafrikanischen Buschmänner*. Leipzig 1925.

11 BURKITT, M. C.: *South Africa's Past in Stone and Paint*. Cambridge 1928.

12 STOW, G. W. and BLEEK, D.: *Rock Paintings in South Africa*. London 1930.

13 BLEEK, D.: 'A Survey of Our Present Knowledge of Rock Paintings in South Africa', *South African Journal of Science*, Vol. XXIX. 1932.

14 WILMAN, M.: *The Rock Engravings of Griqualand West and Bechuanaland, South Africa*. Cambridge 1933.

15 VAN RIET LOWE, C.: 'Prehistoric Art in South Africa', *Official Year Book No. 17 of the Union of South Africa*. 1936.

16 VAN RIET LOWE, C.: *The Distribution of Prehistoric Rock Engravings and Paintings in South Africa*. Pretoria 1952.

17 GOODALL, E.: 'Domestic Animals in Rock Art', *Proceedings of Rhodesian Scientific Association*, Vol. XLI. 1946.

18 GOODALL, E.: 'Some Observations on Rock Paintings Illustrating Burial Rites', *Proceedings of Rhodesian Scientific Association*, Vol. XLI. 1946.

19 FROBENIUS, L.: *Erythraa*. Berlin 1930.

20 FROBENIUS, L.: *Madsimu Dsangara*. Berlin 1931-1932.

21 BATTISS, W.: *The Artists of the Rocks*. Pretoria 1948.

22 GOODWIN, A. J. H. and VAN RIET LOWE, C.: *The Stone Age Cultures of South Africa*. Edinburgh 1929.

23 WILLCOX, A. R.: 'The Status of Smithfield C Reconsidered', *South African Journal of Science*, Vol. LII. 1956.

24 MAINGARD, L. F.: 'The First Contacts of the Dutch with the Bushmen', *South African Journal of Science*, Vol. XXXII. 1935.

25 DAPPER, O.: et al, *Early Cape Hottentots*, Cape Town 1933.

26 WILLCOX, A. R.: 'Hand Imprints in Rock Paintings', *South African Journal of Science*. 1959.

27 WELLS, L. H.: 'The Problem of Middle Stone Age Man in Southern Africa', *Man*. 1959.

28 SINGER, R.: 'The Boskop Race Problem', *Man*. 1958.

29 TOBIAS, P. V.: 'New Evidence and New Views on the Evolution of Man in Africa', *South African Journal of Science*, Vol. LVII. 1961.

30 DRENNAN, M. R.: 'The Principle of Change in Man and Animals and the Role of Feminism or Gynomorphism in it', *South African Archaeological Bulletin*, Vol. XII. 1957.

31 STOW, G. W.: *The Native Races of South Africa*. London 1905.

32 STANFORD, W. E.: 'Statement of Silayi with reference to his life among the Bushmen', *Transactions of the Royal Society of South Africa*. 1909.

33 SCHAPERA, I.: *The Khoisan Peoples of South Africa*. London 1930.

34 WILLCOX, A. R.: *Rock Paintings of the Drakensberg*. London 1956.

35 LICHTENSTEIN, H.: *Travels in Southern Africa*. London 1812-1815.

36 DORNAN, S. S.: 'Notes on the Bushmen of Basutoland', *Transactions of South African Philosophical Society*. 1909.

37 THEAL, G. McCALL: *Records of South Eastern Africa*. London 1898.

38 GOODWIN, A. J. H.: 'Metal Working among the Early Hottentots', *South African Archaeological Bulletin*, Vol. XI. 1956.

39 GALLOWAY, A.: *The Skeletal Remains of Bambandyanalo*. Johannesburg 1959.

40 ELLENBERGER, D. F.:*History of the Basuto*. London 1912.

41 BRYANT, A. T.: *Oldentimes in Zululand and Natal*. London 1929.

42 BUCHANAN, B.: *Pioneer Days in Natal*. Pietermaritzburg 1934.

43 ORPEN, J. M.: *Reminiscences of Life in South Africa*. Durban 1908.

44 ROGERS, G. M.: *I Alone*. Pietermaritzburg 1937.

45 SELOUS, F. C.: *African Nature Notes*. London 1908.

46 THOMAS, E. M.: *The Harmless People*. London 1959.

47 BURCHELL, W. J.: *Travels in the Interior of Southern Africa*. London 1822.

48 ALEXANDER, J.: *Expedition of Discovery into the Interior of Africa*. London 1838.

49 DORNAN, S. S.: *Pygmies and Bushmen of the Kalahari*. London 1925.

50 BLEEK, W. H. I., and LLOYD, L. C.: *Specimens of Bushman Folklore*. London 1911.

51 GALTON, F.: *The Narrative of an Explorer in Tropical South Africa*. London 1853.

52 BARROW, J.: *Travels into the Interior of Southern Africa*. London 1801.

53 POTGIETER, E. F.: *The Disappearing Bushmen of Lake Chrissie*. Pretoria 1955.

54 GOODWIN, A. J. H.: 'Prehistoric Fishing Methods in South Africa', *Antiquity*, Vol. XX. 1946.

55 GOODWIN, A. J. H.: 'A Fishing Scene from East Griqualand', *South African Archaeological Bulletin*, Vol. IV. 1949.

56 BATTISS, W.: 'Prehistoric Fishing Scenes', addendum to 'Sea Animals among the Prehistoric Rock Paintings of Ladybrand' by Henri Breuil, *South African Journal of Science*, Vol. XLI. 1945.

57 VINNICOMBE, P.: 'A Fishing Scene from the Tsoelike River, South-Eastern Basutoland', *South African Archaeological Bulletin*, Vol. XV. 1960.

58 BERGMAN, R. A. M.: *De Sociale Functie der Rotstekeningen*. Amsterdam.

59 CLARK, J. D.: 'Schematic Art', *South African Archaeological Bulletin*, Vol. XIII. 1958.

60 VINNICOMBE, P.: 'A Painting of a Fish-trap on Bamboo Mountain, Underberg District, Southern Natal', *South African Archaeological Bulletin*, Vol. XVI. 1961.

61 ORPEN, J. M.: 'A Glimpse into the Mythology of the Maluti Bushmen', *Cape Monthly Magazine*, (1894) reproduced in *Folklore* 1919.

62 BLEEK, D.: *The Mantis and his Friends*. Cape Town 1923.

63 BLEEK, D.: 'Beliefs and Customs of the Ixam Bushmen, Part V, The Rain', *Bantu Studies*. 1933.

64 WILLCOX, A. R.: 'Art and Language', Essay in *South African P.E.N. Year Book*. 1954.

65 BREUIL, H.: *Afrique*, Cahier d'Art. Paris 1931.

66 WILLCOX, A. R.: 'The Classification of Rock Paintings', *South African Journal of Science*, Vol. LIII. 1957.

67 WILLCOX, A. R.: 'The Shaded Polychrome Paintings of South Africa: their Distribution, Origin and Age', *South African Archaeological Bulletin*, Vol. X. 1955.

68 TOWNLEY JOHNSON, R., RABINOWITZ, H. and SIEFF, P.: *Rock Paintings of the South-West Cape*. Cape Town 1959.

69 ELLENBERGER, V.: *La Fin Tragique des Bushman*. Paris 1953.

70 WILLCOX, A. R.: 'Hand Imprints in Rock Paintings', *South African Journal of Science*. 1959.

71 RUDNER, J.: 'The Brandberg and its Archaeological Remains', *Journal of the South-West African Scientific Society*, Vol. XII. 1957.

72 RUDNER, I. and J.: 'Who Were the Artists?', *South African Archaeological Bulletin*, Vol. XIV. 1959.

73 WILLCOX, A. R.: 'Who Were the Artists? Another Opinion', *South African Archaeological Bulletin*, Vol. XV. 1960.

74 THOM, H. B.: (Ed.) *Journal of van Riebeeck*. Cape Town 1952.

75 TOBIAS, P. V.: 'Physical Anthropology and the Somatic Origins of the Hottentots', *African Studies*, Vol. XIV. 1955.

76 LOUW, J. T.: *Prehistory of the Matjes River Rock Shelter*. Bloemfontein 1960.

77 GOODWIN, A. J. H., DRENNAN, M. R. and SCHOFIELD, J. F.: 'Archaeology of the Oakhurst Shelter, George', *Transactions of the Royal Society of South Africa*, Vol. XXV. 1938.

78 FITZSIMONS, F. W.: 'The Cliff Dwellers of Zitzikama', *South African Journal of Science*, Vol. XX. 1923.

79 WILLCOX, A. R.: 'Stone Cultures and Prehistoric Art in South Africa', *South African Journal of Science*, Vol. LIII, 1956.

80 SCHWEIGER, A.: 'The Bushman Caves of Keilands', *Catholic Magazine for South Africa*, Vol. XXIII. 1912.

81 SCHWEIGER, A.: 'Neuentdeckte Buschmannmalereien in der Cape-Provinz, Südostafrika', *Anthropos*, Vol. 8. 1913.

82 DART, R. A.: 'The Historical Succession of Cultural Impacts upon South Africa', *Nature*. 1925.

83 WALTON, J.: 'Kaross-clad Figures from South African Rock Paintings', *South African Archaeological Bulletin*, Vol. VI. 1951.

84 BREUIL, H.: 'The Influence of Classical Civilisations on the Cave Paintings of South Africa', *Proceedings of the First Pan-African Congress on Prehistory.* 1947.

85 BREUIL, H.: 'Some Foreigners in the Frescoes on Rocks in Southern Africa', *South African Archaeological Bulletin*, Vol. IV. 1949.

86 BREUIL, H.: 'Sea Animals amongst the Prehistoric Rock Paintings of Ladybrand', *South African Journal of Science*, Vol. XLI. 1944.

87 WELLS, L. H.: 'Marine Animals in a Rock Painting near Fouriesburg', *South African Journal of Science*, Vol. XLII. 1946.

88 WILLCOX, A. R.: 'Marine Animals in Rock Paintings', *South African Journal of Science*, Vol. LVIII. 1962.

89 BREUIL, H.: 'Carbon Test and South West African Paintings', *South African Archaeological Bulletin*, Vol. IX. 1954.

90 MARTIN, H., and MASON, R.: 'The Test Trench in the Phillips Cave, Ameib, Erongo Mountain, South West Africa', *South African Archaeological Bulletin*, Vol. IX. 1954.

91 WALTON, J.: 'South West African Rock Paintings and the Triple Curved Bow', *South African Archaeological Bulletin*, Vol. IX. 1954.

92 DART, R. A.: 'Rock Engravings in Southern Africa and Some Clues to their Significance', *South African Journal of Science*, Vol. XXVIII. 1931.

93 CLARK, J. D.: 'The Newly Discovered Natchikufu Culture of Northern Rhodesia', *South African Archaeological Bulletin*, Vol. V. 1950.

94 DART, R. A.: 'Rhodesian Engravers, Painters and Pigment Miners of the Fifth Millennium B.C.' *South African Archaeological Bulletin*, Vol. VIII. 1953.

95 CLARK, J. D.: 'The Chifubwa Stream Rock Shelter, Solwezi, Northern Rhodesia', *South African Archaeological Bulletin*, Vol. XIII. 1958.

96 GOODALL, E., COOKE, C. K., CLARK, J. D., and SUMMERS, R.: *The Prehistoric Rock Art of the Federation of Rhodesia and Nyasaland.* 1959.

97 HAHN, T.: 'Felsgiechen der Buschmänner', *Berliner Gesellschaft für Anthropologie, etc.*, 1879.

98 DORNAN, S. S. 'The Tati Bushmen (Masarwas) and their Language', *Journal of the Royal Anthropological Society*, Vol. XLVII. 1917.

99 WILLCOX, A. R.: 'Australian and South African Rock Art Compared', *South African Archaeological Bulletin*, Vol. XIV. 1959.

100 GOODWIN, A. J. H.: *Vosburg: Its Petroglyphs.* Cape Town 1936.

101 VAN RIET LOWE, C.: 'Prehistoric Rock Engravings in the Vaal River Basin', *Transactions of the Royal Society of South Africa.* Vol. XXIV. 1937.

102 VAN RIET LOWE, C.: 'Prehistoric Rock Engravings in the Krugersdorp – Rustenburg Area of the Transvaal', *South African Journal of Science*, Vol. XLI. 1945.

103 CHAPLIN, J. A.: 'The Munwa Stream Rock-Engravings', *South African Archaeological Bulletin*, Vol. XIV. 1959.

104 TEIXIERA, M. A. DE PIMENTAL: 'Rock Peckings from Angola', *South African Archaeological Bulletin*, Vol. VII. 1952.

105 LASZLO, A. E.: 'An Expedition to Rock Carvings in Southern Angola', *South African Archaeological Bulletin*, Vol. X. 1955.

106 JEFFREYS, M. D. W.: 'Doodling at Forest Vale and Redan', *South African Archaeological Bulletin*, Vol. VII. 1953.

107 VAN RIET LOWE, C.: 'The Rock Engravings of Driekopseiland'. *Proceedings of the Second Pan-African Congress on Prehistory*. 1952.

108 WILLCOX, A. R.: 'Another Rock Slide', *South African Archaeological Bulletin*, Vol. XVI. 1961.

109 HOLM, E.: 'Uitgestorwe Diere in ons Voorhistoriese Kuns', *South African Archaeological Bulletin*, Vol. XI. 1956.

110 DUNNE, E. J.: *The Bushman*. London 1931.

111 LUSCHAN, F. VON: 'Bildende Kunst bei den Buschmänner', *Die Umschau*. Frankfurt-am-Main 1907.

112 VAN RIET LOWE, C.: 'Pinturas Rupertres e la Cultura do Zimbaue', *Bol. Societe de Estudos do Colonia de Moçambique*. 1948.

113 BLEEK, W. H. I.: *A Brief Account of Bushmen Folklore*, London 1875.

114 *Cape of Good Hope Report and Proceedings of the Government Commission on Native Laws and Customs*, Appendix 1 – Pondomise Customs.

115 HOW, M. W.: *The Mountain Bushmen of Basutoland*. Pretoria 1962.

116 PERINGUEY, L.: 'On Rock Engravings of Animals and the Human Figure (Second Note)', *Transactions of the South African Philosophical Society*, Vol. XVIII 1909.

117 SCHOONRAAD, M.: 'Rock Painting Depicting Prehistoric Fishing Found near Maclear', *South African Journal of Science*, Vol. LVIII. 1962.

118 CLARK, J. D.: *The Prehistory of Southern Africa*. London 1959.

119 WILLCOX, A. R.: 'Painted Petroglyphs at Balerno in the Limpopo Valley, Transvaal. *South African Journal of Science*, Vol. LIX. 1963.

120 WILLCOX, A. R.: 'The Non-Representational Petroglyphs of South Africa'. *South African Journal of Science*, in press.

121 MACQUARRIE, J. W. (Ed.) *The Reminiscences of Sir Walter Stanford*, Vol. 2, 1962.

122 FREAN, C. J.: 'A Pioneer Remembers', *South African Archaeological Bulletin*, Vol. XVI 1961.

Index

Q)